WEAVING INNOVATIONS
from the Bateman Collection

Robyn Spady, Nancy A. Tracy, and Marjorie Fiddler

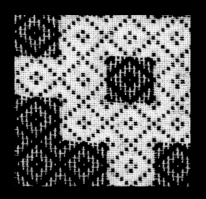 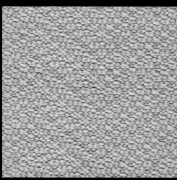 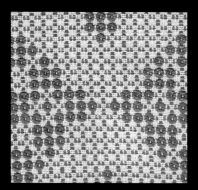

Foreword by Madelyn van der Hoogt

4880 Lower Valley Road • Atglen, PA 19310

Other Schiffer Books on Related Subjects:

Weaving Designs by Bertha Gray Hayes: Miniature Overshot Patterns,
Norma Smayda, Gretchen White, Jody Brown, & Katharine Schelleng,
ISBN 978-0-7643-3246-3

Weaver's Study Course: Sourcebook for Ideas and Techniques, Else
Regensteiner, ISBN 978-0-88740-112-1

Norwegian Pick-Up Bandweaving, Heather Torgenrud,
ISBN 978-0-7643-4751-1

Cover design by RoS
Type set in Chalet-NewYorkNineteenEighty/Times New Roman

ISBN: 978-0-7643-4991-1

Printed in China

Published by Schiffer Publishing, Ltd.
4880 Lower Valley Road
Atglen, PA 19310
Phone: (610) 593-1777; Fax: (610) 593-2002
E-mail: Info@schifferbooks.com

For our complete selection of fine books on this and related subjects,
please visit our website at www.schifferbooks.com. You may also write
for a free catalog.

This book may be purchased from the publisher. Please try your bookstore
first.

We are always looking for people to write books on new and related
subjects. If you have an idea for a book, please contact us at proposals@
schifferbooks.com.

Schiffer Publishing's titles are available at special discounts for bulk
purchases for sales promotions or premiums. Special editions, including
personalized covers, corporate imprints, and excerpts can be created in
large quantities for special needs. For more information, contact the
publisher.

CONTENTS

Dr. William G. Bateman and his eight-shaft table loom

FOREWORD

When we first start to weave, most of us are overwhelmed by all there is to learn. We are faced with an unfamiliar vocabulary—almost a complete new language—as we begin to acquire our weaving libraries. Only after many warps and much reading and re-reading (along with frustration and error) do we begin to understand how weave structures work. We learn to distinguish twill from plain weave; we discover lace weaves, summer and winter, overshot, and the versatile design potential of twills. As most weavers have done before us, we assume that the weave structures we find in handweaving literature (representing weaving traditions from all over the world) comprise most, if not all, of what's possible. It is often even said that there is nothing "new" in weaving, that it is the combination of weave structure, yarn type, and color interaction that makes a particular cloth unique.

Dr. William G. Bateman did not get that message. Moreover, when he began weaving in the mid-1900s, handweaving literature was much more limited than it is today. It's only my guess, but his main sources were likely to have been Mary Meigs Atwater, Harriet Tidball, Berta Frey, and Marguerite Davison. The pattern weaves most familiar to him were probably overshot, twills, Atwater-Bronson lace, M's and O's, and summer and winter. Most of us are satisfied with understanding a structure enough to use it. Not so for Dr. Bateman.

Dr. Bateman took the weave structures from these sources in completely new directions. In each of the weave structures he developed (Multiple Tabby Weaves; Bateman Blends; Park, Boulevard, and Chevron Weaves; Extended and Divided Twills), he extended the basic principle of a known weave in ways no one had remotely dreamed of before. In most cases, his new weaves allow four or more threading blocks on eight shafts. The shaft order within each block can usually be shifted to make additional variations, showing new textures within each pattern block. Adding threads to each block adds even more potential for varying the threading order and the resulting texture and/or pattern. Some of his weaves are woven with a single weft (the twills and Multiple Tabby); most can be woven with either a single weft or two wefts—one for tabby, one for pattern. The possible treadling variations are so many, in fact, that the resulting interlacements often defy classification.

Knowing that he wove 389 warps (each numbered) with six to twelve samples on each of them (also numbered) *after* retiring as a professor of chemistry is beyond daunting. He was a master of permutations and combinations, and it would be marvelous to know more about how he worked and how he thought. It is tantalizing to imagine what he might have done with more shafts (he worked on a relatively primitive eight-shaft table loom) and, most especially, what he would have done with a computer. Instead, he moved lever after lever, shed by shed, after figuring out—on paper—the threading for each warp and the treadling for each sample.

We are lucky, however, that he did work this way, as time-consuming as it must have been for him. As a result, we have inherited the actual woven fabrics instead of reams of computer printouts. We are especially lucky that with the publication of this book, we can see so many of his fabric samples in color. The black-and-white photos in the Shuttle Craft Guild monographs are certainly intriguing, but the fabrics in these pages will inspire you to try his amazing innovations on your loom—and maybe even use his methods to invent some of your own.

Madelyn van der Hoogt

ACKNOWLEDGMENTS

The authors would like to acknowledge the contributions from the following people:

Mimi Anderson
Barbara Doyon
Sandra Swarbrick
Bill Way

INTRODUCTION

The Bateman Legacy

Dr. William G. Bateman developed an interest in handweaving at a young age. When he was five years old he attended a kindergarten in Salt Lake City, Utah. As he returned home from school, he regularly passed by a weaving shop where the rhythm of the beaters going thump, thump, thump attracted his attention. Many years later, he told his daughter that he had cleared a small place on the window to see what was causing the noise. The peephole was used almost daily to satisfy this small boy's curiosity as he watched the weavers at work.

It was many years later, when his wife Belle Bateman assisted Mary Meigs Atwater at a summer workshop, that Dr. Bateman had an opportunity to learn more about weaving. However, additional years were to pass before he could start to satisfy his curiosity with a concentrated study of weaving. Even though Dr. Bateman's training and profession were unrelated to the textile arts, his intellectual curiosity and scientific discipline were reflected in his approach to the study of weaving. He earned BA and MA degrees at Stanford University and a PhD in physiological chemistry from Yale. He taught at Stanford and at Pei-Yang University in Tiensen, China, then returned to the United States to become professor of chemistry and chairman of the premedical department at the Graduate School of Montana State University in Missoula. After twenty-five years at that institution, he retired and moved with his wife to Seattle to be near their daughter, Jane. It was after his move to Seattle that he finally began his exploration of weaving.

The creative arts had always been an influence in Dr. Bateman's life. His family included many artists who were engaged in music, painting, writing, and the crafts. Music and writing were his life-long leisure activities. He was a pianist and composer of music and he wrote stories for the entertainment of his family. His wife was a painter and head of the art department at Montana State University. His oldest daughter, Jane Bateman Henke, was also a painter, teacher, and sculptor. Both his wife and daughter gave him advice on color and design in his weaving and at times, helped him prepare the loom for weaving.

Originally, Dr. Bateman intended to prepare a weavers' reference collection that would be used for classes in weaving, textiles, and design, and as study materials for weavers' organizations. He planned to weave samples and variations of all the known weaves. Using an eight-shaft Missouri table loom, he produced over eight cardboard file storage boxes of samples, beginning with plain weave and progressing through overshot, twill, crackle, tied weaves, weaver-controlled weaves, and others. As he progressed with his plan to document the unit weaves, his curiosity and inventiveness led him to variations on established weaves and to the discovery and creation of new weave systems. For instance, the Multiple Tabby weave was an extension of the M's and O's weave, but the Boulevard weave is considered new because a thorough search of hand weaving literature uncovered no reference to such a weave.

Before many samples were made, he started building collections: one for the home economics department of Montana State University and one for himself. He also shared his samples by preparing traveling exhibits. These were circulated and they traveled throughout the United States, Canada, and to some foreign countries during the 1950s and early 1960s.

The Bateman Collection

Dr. Bateman kept records of each of his warps and all of the samples woven on these warps. He numbered his warps and each sample on that warp. At the present time, it is unknown precisely how many samples he wove. There were a total of 389 warps with six to twelve samples on each one.

Dr. Bateman's personal collection and manuscript were passed down to Virginia Harvey by the Bateman family with the hope it would be made available to weavers. Virginia, with the help of Luise Ziegler, worked for ten years on editing, verifying, and mounting the materials in her possession. She published six monographs based on Dr. Bateman's manuscript: *Multiple Tabby Weaves; Bateman Blend Weaves; Park Weaves; Boulevard, Chevron, and Combination Weaves; Extended Divided Twill Weaves;* and *Extended Manifold Weaves.* In the early 1990s, Virginia passed along the materials in her possession to the Seattle Weavers' Guild.

Today, the majority of Dr. Bateman's samples are included in collections owned by the Seattle Weavers' Guild and Montana State University. There are currently 1,473 mounted samples in the Seattle Weavers' Guild collection.

The Seattle Weavers' Guild has been interested in sharing Dr. Bateman's work since it acquired its collection; however, the magnitude of nearly 1,500 samples was daunting. To create a manageable scope, a group of samples were selected and are presented in this book. They were chosen based on a number of factors, including their aesthetic appeal and their unique interpretation of a particular weave or threading.

The samples in this book are only a portion of the samples Dr. Bateman wove and represent some of the most innovative weaves he created. They provide a peek into the breadth of the work Dr. Bateman completed in not only his own weaves, but also more traditional weaves not previously published.

A Few Words from the Authors

The samples in this book are Dr. Bateman's original samples and include the yarns and setts he outlined in his documentation over sixty years ago. All of the samples Dr. Bateman wove were completed on an eight-shaft Missouri table loom. This is important to keep in mind when reviewing many of the samples since some require many more treadles than floor looms typically have.

The samples in the book have been organized into different weave groups. Within each weave group, the samples are presented in chronological order. The sample assignment Dr. Bateman designated is shown for each sample. The threading for the warp is shown first and is then followed by samples woven on it. We have made an effort to provide the information for each sample as it was woven; however, all of the drafts have been adapted to conform to the following:

- Rising shed floor loom
- Threadings are read right-to-left
- Threading blocks and threading profiles are also presented right-to-left to be consistent with the threading sequences
- Treadlings are read top-down

While working on this book, we felt it was important for readers to know the following:

- Drafts are presented in color. This helps emphasize the logic of sequences, the use of color, the interleaving of pattern, and more for many of the samples.

- Not all of Dr. Bateman's samples are created equal. Some samples have a threading repeat of five ends, while other samples have significantly longer threading repeats. The same is true for treadling sequences. As odd as this may look in the book, it presents the wide range of weaves Dr. Bateman explored.

- In the manuscript of his work, Dr. Bateman only details sample information and does not present his inspiration, design approach, or objective for a particular sample or sample set.

- Many samples use irregular tabby sequences. Also, for some of the threading sequences, a true plain weave is not possible.

- Dr. Bateman's samples survived two fires many years ago. As a result, some samples were damaged and a complete image of the sample is not possible.

- Information about the samples is taken from the documentation in Dr. Bateman's manuscript. This results in limited information about many of the yarns used, including size, color, and fiber content. In addition, a color term he used may not appear consistent with the actual color of the yarn.

- Duplication of his samples may be challenging because of different yarn properties, sample width, or because of a difference in beat. We hope the samples here serve as inspiration to many weavers and will be interpreted in different setts, colors, and yarns.

After working on this compilation of Dr. Bateman's samples, we recognize there are more questions than answers about his work. We can only speculate; however, we hope that by sharing these samples with others, we will derive further insight into his work.

Robyn Spady   Nancy A. Tracy   Marjorie Fiddler

SECTION ONE
BATEMAN WEAVES

It's difficult to separate the Bateman weaves from each other because most of them are related and all of them were developed by Dr. Bateman. They differ from other weave systems because most of them do not have a traditional sequence that gives a classic texture or pattern.

All of Dr. Bateman's weaves may be considered unit weaves because they are composed of blocks that can be drafted from a profile. Classifying Dr. Bateman's original work is challenging. He took his original blocks of each of the systems and contracted, extended, or transposed parts of the block(s) or expanded the entire block until some of the blocks bear little resemblance to the original version.

Several of Dr. Bateman's weaves would fit into another class, in addition to the unit weaves. For example, Extended Divided Twill and Extended Manifold Twill would fit in the twill class. The drafts of Multiple Tabby weaves would fit with its relative, the M's and O's weave. The Bateman Blend, Park, Boulevard, and Chevron weaves are the only weaves that fit in the Bateman unit weave class.

In this section, each sample warp shows the following:

- Number assigned by Dr. Bateman
- Weave description
- Yarns and colors used for the warp ends
- Sett
- Threading blocks
- Threading profile
- Complete threading repeat

For each sample, the following information is noted:

- Number and sub-number assigned by Dr. Bateman
- Yarns and colors used for weft picks
- Tie-up
- Plain weave and tabby treadles when applicable
- Treadling sequence with treadling blocks shown by brackets
- Treadling profile if the treadling blocks are not woven in consecutive order

Bateman Blend Weaves

One of the weaves developed by Dr. Bateman is a unit weave created from a blend of the Atwater-Bronson and the single two-tie (aka Summer and Winter) unit weaves. Dr. Bateman originally called this system the At-Win weave; however Harriett Tidball changed it to Bateman Blend.

Blocks for Atwater-Bronson lace require six ends.

Atwater-Bronson threading blocks

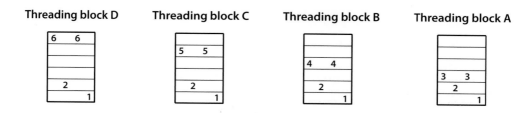

Threading block D	Threading block C	Threading block B	Threading block A

Blocks for Summer and Winter, a single two-tie weave structure, require only four ends per block.

Summer and Winter threading blocks

Threading block D	Threading block C	Threading block B	Threading block A

All Bateman Blend blocks are composed of three elements:

1. The tie group. The term "tie group" is used by Dr. Bateman to describe the first two ends of the threading block.
2. The tie downs on shafts one and two not included in the tie group.
3. The pattern ends. These are all warp ends not part of the tie group or tie downs.

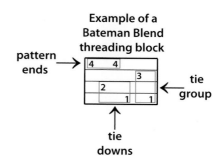

Example of a Bateman Blend threading block

pattern ends →

tie group ←

tie downs ↑

Dr. Bateman did not create a single Bateman Blend block. In fact, he created many variations. The most significant variation between the Bateman Blend blocks was the rearrangement of the tie downs.

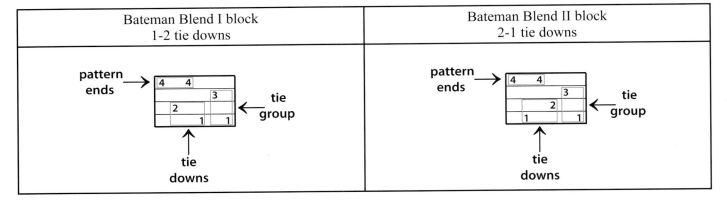

Bateman Blend I block 1-2 tie downs	Bateman Blend II block 2-1 tie downs

Below is an example of four Bateman Blend threading blocks, A through D, based on the Bateman Blend I 1-2 tie down sequence.

Bateman Blend threading blocks

Even though the Bateman Blend weave samples woven by Dr. Bateman were limited to eight shafts, blocks may be expanded for more shafts. The number of ends in a Bateman Blend threading block varied in size from six-end to twelve-end blocks. The number of ends may be contracted, expanded, or even reconfigured. Below are examples of different Bateman Blend threading blocks.

Bateman Blend threading blocks - contracted

For more information about Bateman Blend weaves, refer to Harvey, Virginia I., *Bateman Blend Weaves, Based on Dr. William G. Bateman's Manuscript*, Shuttle Craft Guild Monograph 36 (Freeland, WA: HTH Publishers, 1982).

Bateman Blend threading blocks - expanded

Warp 163

Weave: Eight-shaft Bateman Blend
Sett: 37½ epi
Warp: ☐ Aptex California lime

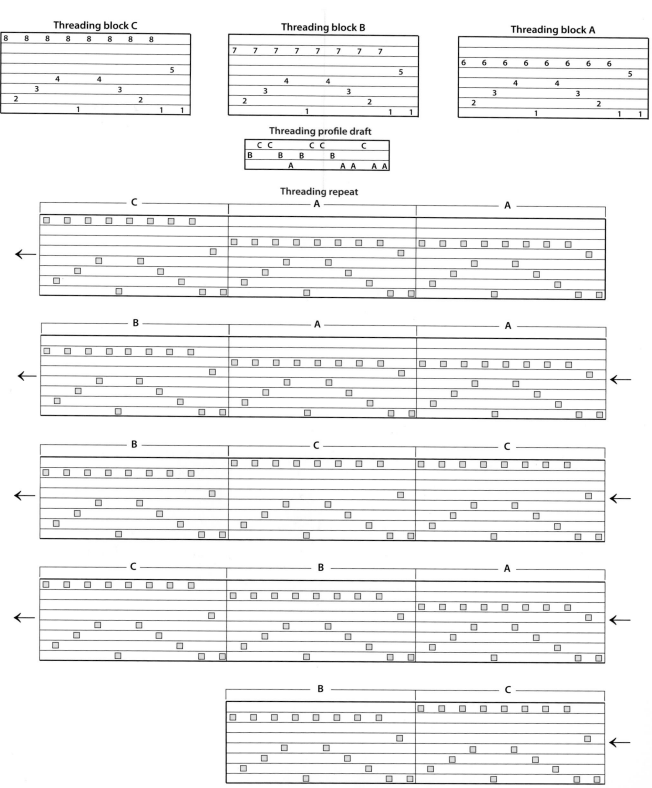

Threading block C

| 8 | 8 | 8 | 8 | 8 | 8 | 8 | 8 |

Threading block B

| 7 | 7 | 7 | 7 | 7 | 7 | 7 | 7 |

Threading block A

| 6 | 6 | 6 | 6 | 6 | 6 | 6 | 6 |

Threading profile draft

Threading repeat

163-3

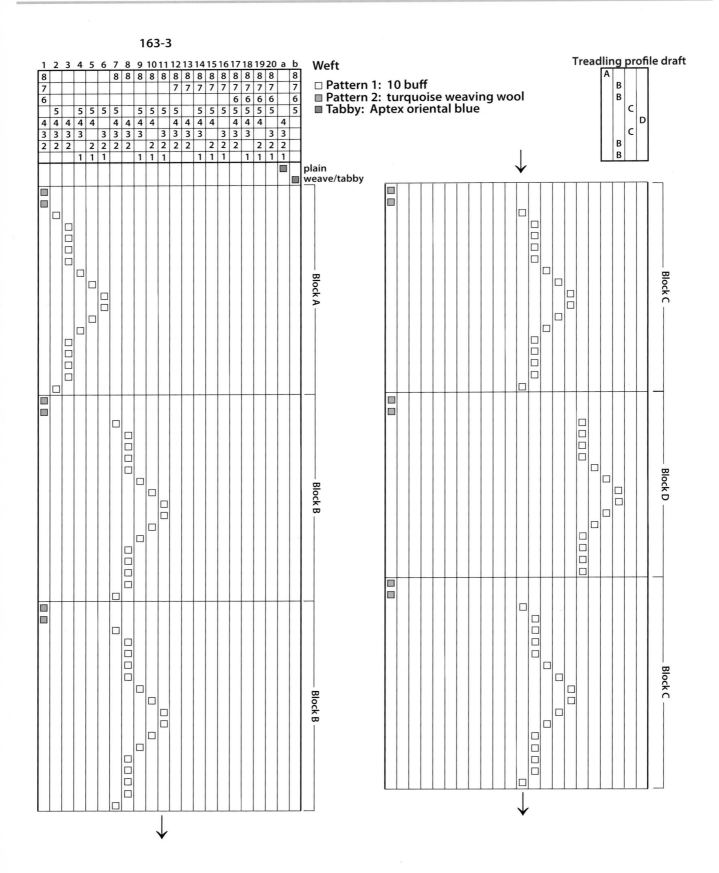

Weft

☐ Pattern 1: 10 buff
🟦 Pattern 2: turquoise weaving wool
⬛ Tabby: Aptex oriental blue

Treadling profile draft

163-3

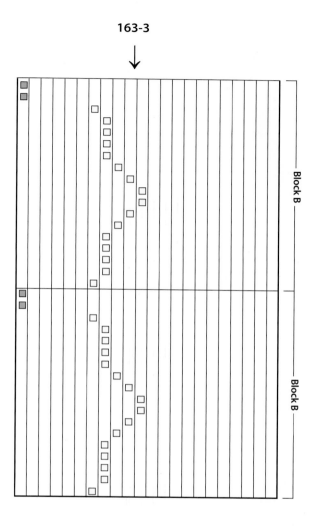

Block B

Block B

Warp 263F

Weave: Seven-shaft Bateman Blend
Sett: 30 epi
Warp: ☐ 20/2 dark ecru

Threading block D

7	7		7
			3
		2	
1	1		1

Threading block C

6		6	6	
				3
			2	
1		1		1

Threading block B

5		5	5	
				3
			2	
1		1		1

Threading block A

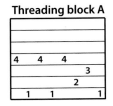

Threading profile draft

			D
		C	
	B		
			A

Threading repeat

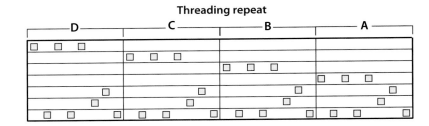

263F-1

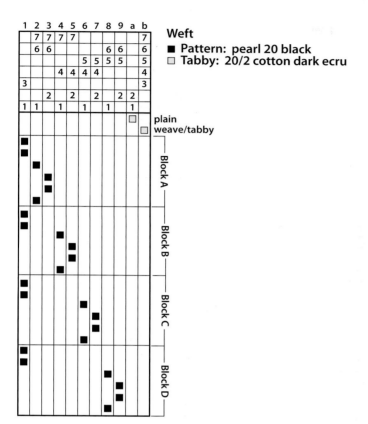

Weft

■ Pattern: pearl 20 black
□ Tabby: 20/2 cotton dark ecru

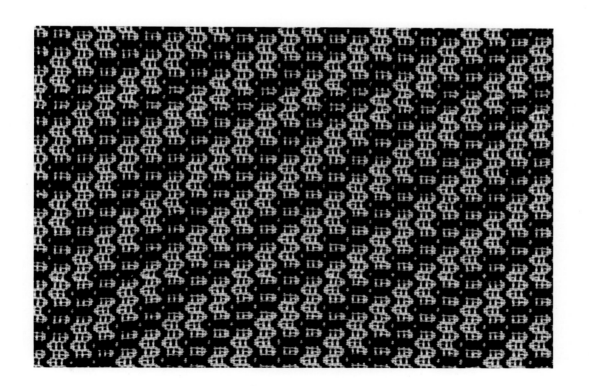

263F-2

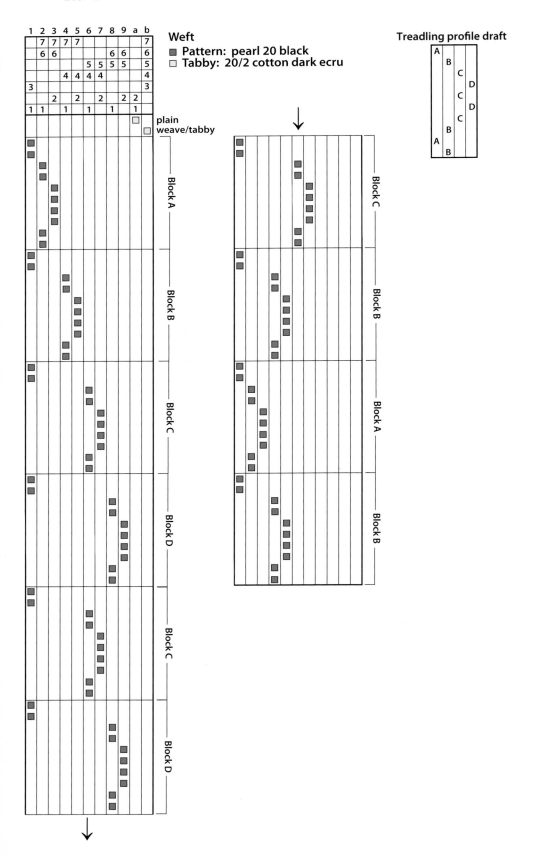

Weft
- ■ Pattern: pearl 20 black
- ☐ Tabby: 20/2 cotton dark ecru

Treadling profile draft

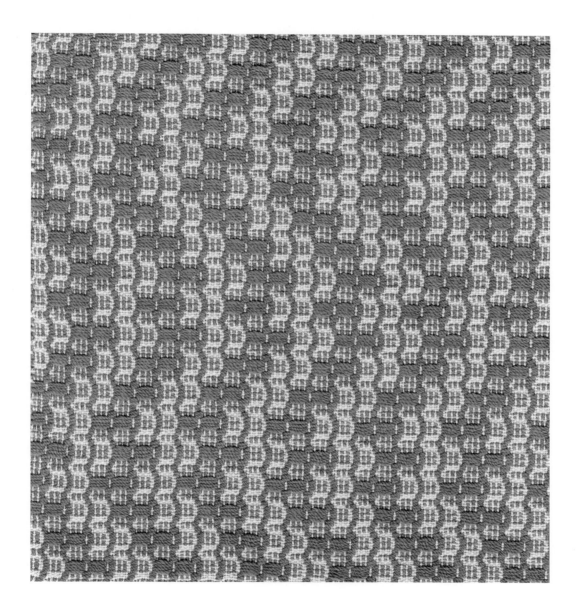

263F-3

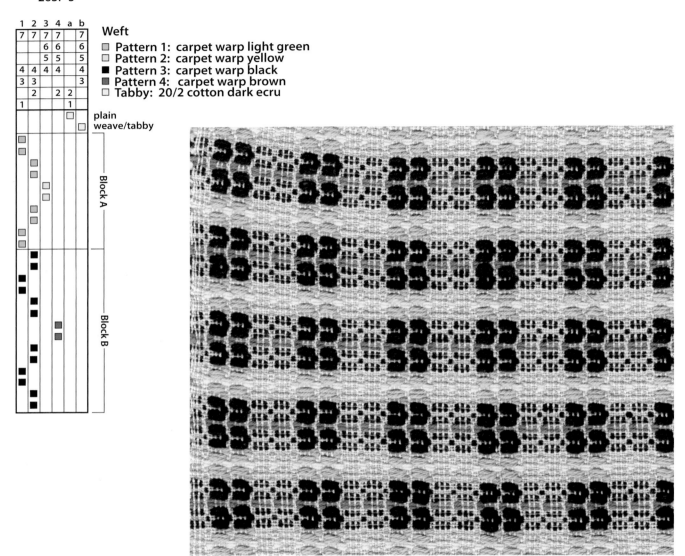

Weft

- ☐ **Pattern 1:** carpet warp light green
- ☐ **Pattern 2:** carpet warp yellow
- ■ **Pattern 3:** carpet warp black
- ■ **Pattern 4:** carpet warp brown
- ☐ **Tabby:** 20/2 cotton dark ecru

plain weave/tabby

Block A

Block B

263F-4

1	2	3	4	a	b
7			7		7
6		6			6
	5	5			5
		4		4		4
					3
				2	
1	1	1	1	1	

Weft
- ◻ Pattern: light rust worsted wool
- ☐ Tabby: 20/2 cotton dark ecru

plain weave

Block A

Block B

Block C

Block D

Note: Due to the atypical tabby used for this sample (e.g., all tabby picks are done on the same treadle), the weft picks for both the pattern and tabby are shown in the treadling sequence.

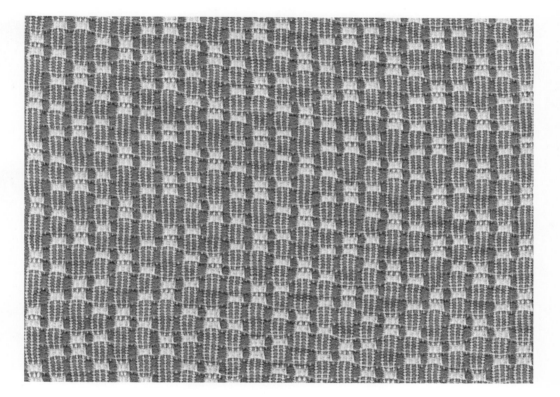

263F-5

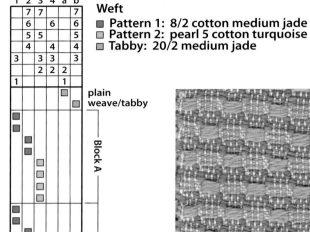

Weft
- Pattern 1: 8/2 cotton medium jade
- Pattern 2: pearl 5 cotton turquoise
- Tabby: 20/2 medium jade

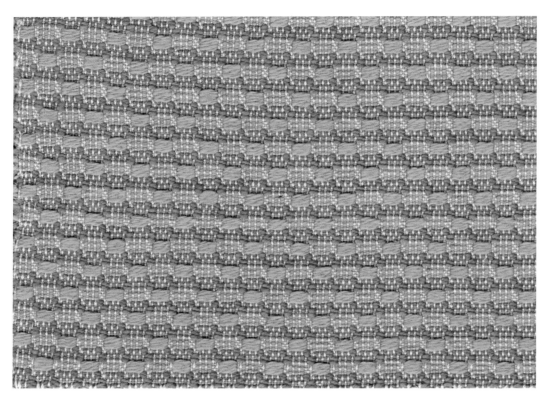

Warp 290

Weave: Seven-shaft Bateman Blend
Sett: 30 epi
Warp: ■ Pearl 20 aqua

Threading block D

4	4	4	4	
				3
2			2	
		1	1	1

Threading block C

5	5	5	5	
				3
2			2	
		1	1	1

Threading block B

6	6	6	6	
				3
2			2	
		1	1	1

Threading block A

7	7	7	7	
				3
2			2	
		1	1	1

Threading profile draft

D			
	C		
		B	
			A

Threading repeat

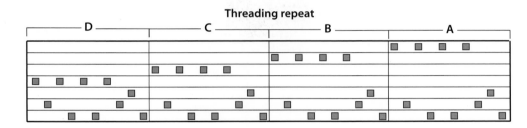

290-1

	1	2	3	4	5	6	7	8	9	a	b
		7	7	7	7						7
			6	6	6	6					6
					5	5	5	5			5
		4	4					4	4		4
	3										3
			2		2		2		2	2	
	1	1		1		1		1			1

Weft

□ Pattern: 10/3 cotton lily green
■ Tabby: green

plain weave/tabby

Block A

Block B

Block C

Block D

290-3

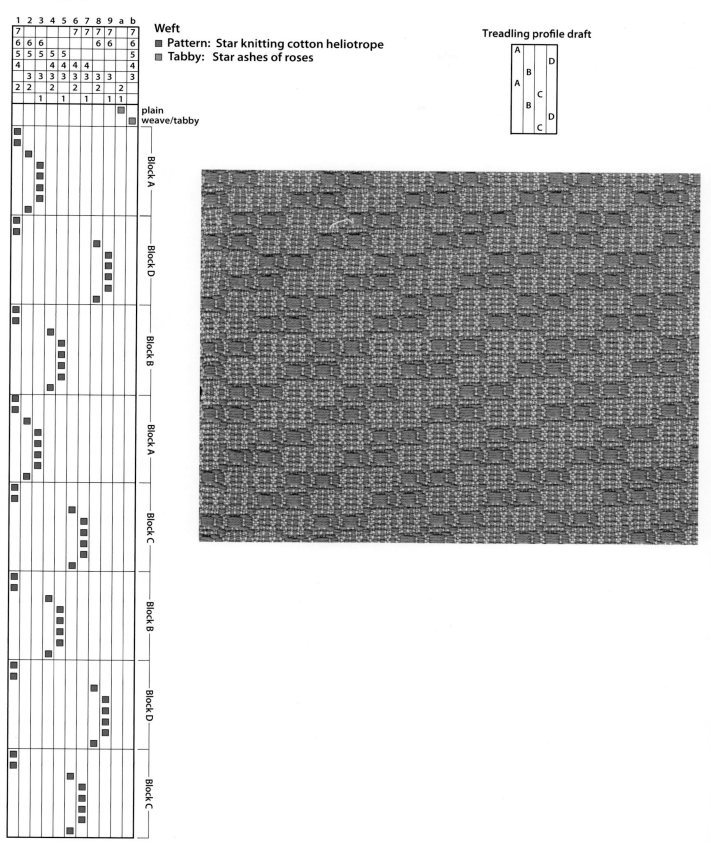

Weft
- ■ Pattern: Star knitting cotton heliotrope
- ■ Tabby: Star ashes of roses

Treadling profile draft

plain weave/tabby

Block A

Block D

Block B

Block A

Block C

Block B

Block D

Block C

290-4

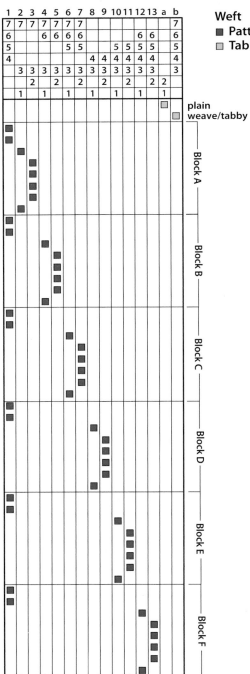

	1	2	3	4	5	6	7	8	9	10	11	12	13	a	b
7	7	7	7	7	7	7	7								7
6	6			6	6	6	6				6	6			6
5	5				5	5			5	5	5	5			5
4	4							4	4	4	4	4	4		4
		3	3	3	3	3	3	3	3	3	3	3	3		3
			2		2		2		2		2		2	2	
		1		1		1		1		1		1		1	1

plain weave/tabby

Block A
Block B
Block C
Block D
Block E
Block F

Weft
■ **Pattern:** pearl 5 Copenhagen blue
□ **Tabby:** Star rose cendre

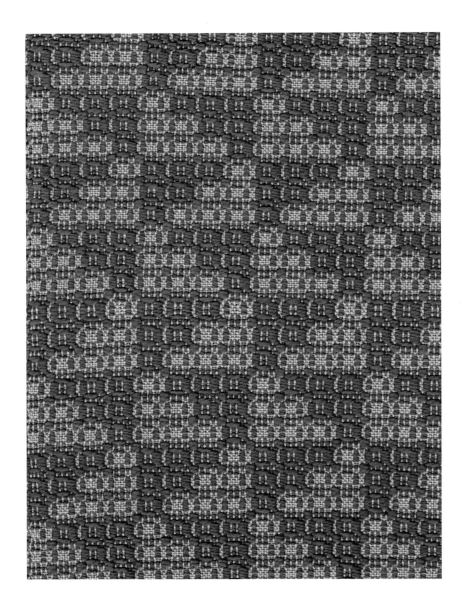

290-5

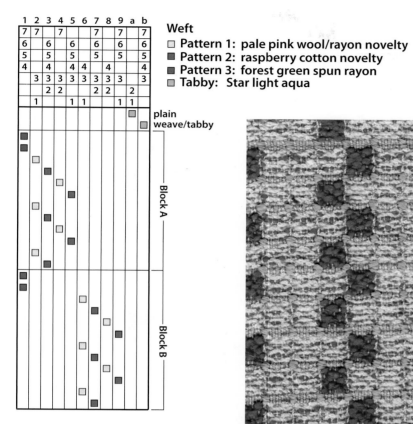

Weft

☐ **Pattern 1:** pale pink wool/rayon novelty
■ **Pattern 2:** raspberry cotton novelty
■ **Pattern 3:** forest green spun rayon
☐ **Tabby:** Star light aqua

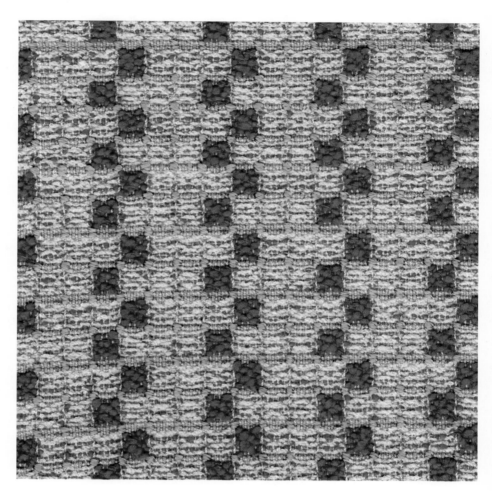

Sample Set on Warp #100

While working on this book and verifying the drafts for the samples, it was discovered on warp #100, a five-block Bateman Blend threading, that Dr. Bateman incorporated pick-up techniques to create his samples. Since describing pick-up techniques are outside the scope of this book, we discussed excluding the samples from the book. Upon further review and discussion, it was decided to adapt them to threadings that require more than eight shafts.

Warp 100-1 (adapted for loom-controlled weave)

Weave: Fourteen-shaft Bateman Blend
Sett: 30 epi
Warp: ☐ 20/2 natural mercerized cotton

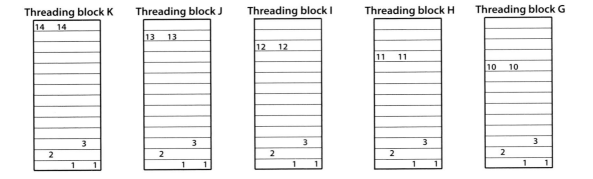

Threading block F — 9 9 · 3 · 2 · 1 1
Threading block E — 8 8 · 3 · 2 · 1 1
Threading block D — 7 7 · 3 · 2 · 1 1
Threading block C — 6 6 · 3 · 2 · 1 1
Threading block B — 5 5 · 3 · 2 · 1 1
Threading block A — 4 4 · 3 · 2 · 1 1

Threading block K — 14 14 · 3 · 2 · 1 1
Threading block J — 13 13 · 3 · 2 · 1 1
Threading block I — 12 12 · 3 · 2 · 1 1
Threading block H — 11 11 · 3 · 2 · 1 1
Threading block G — 10 10 · 3 · 2 · 1 1

Threading profile draft

K
J   J
I   I
H   H
G   G
F   F
E   E
D   D
C   C
B   B
A   A

Warp 100-1 (adapted for loom-controlled weave)
(continued)

Threading repeat

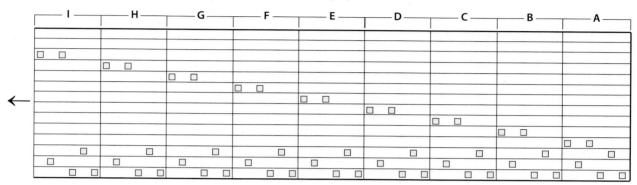

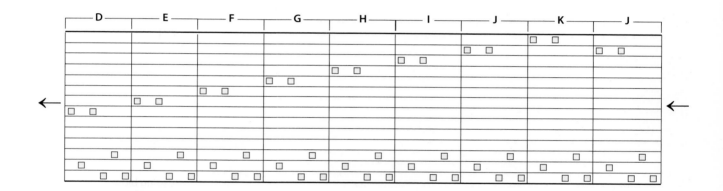

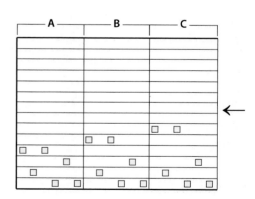

100-1

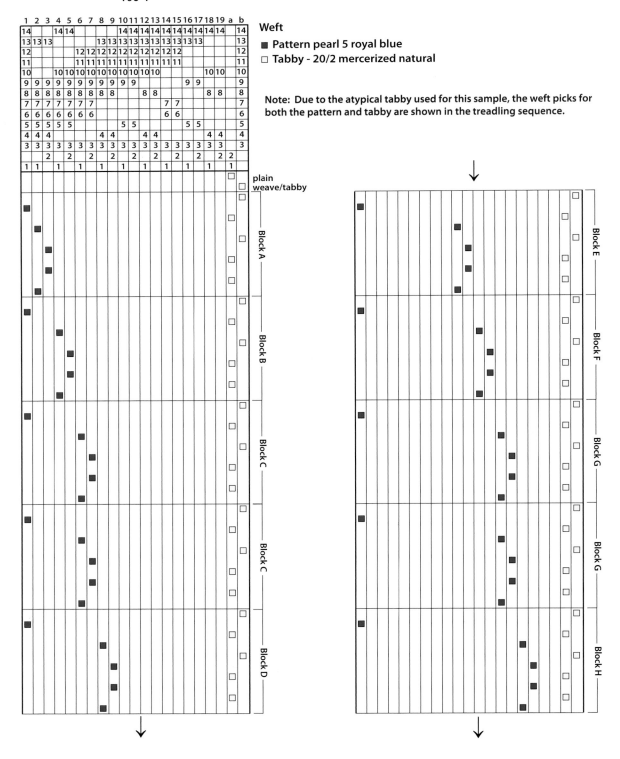

Weft

■ Pattern pearl 5 royal blue

□ Tabby - 20/2 mercerized natural

Note: Due to the atypical tabby used for this sample, the weft picks for both the pattern and tabby are shown in the treadling sequence.

plain weave/tabby

Block A

Block B

Block C

Block C

Block D

Block E

Block F

Block G

Block G

Block H

100-1 (continued)

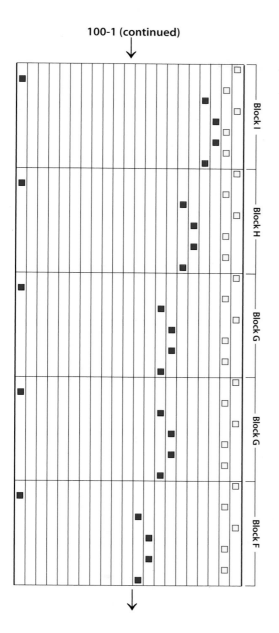

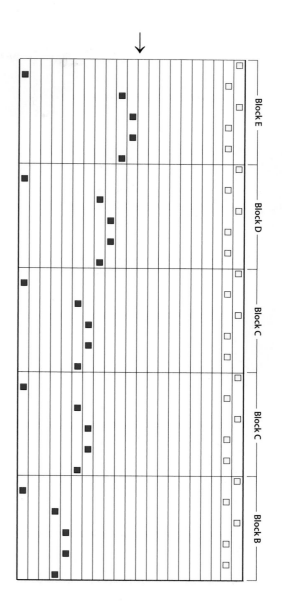

Treadling profile draft

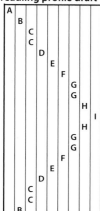

Warp 100-2 and 100-6 (adapted for loom-controlled weave)

Weave: Fifteen-shaft Bateman Blend
Sett: 30 epi
Warp: ☐ 20/2 natural mercerized cotton

Threading block F | Threading block E | Threading block D | Threading block C | Threading block B | Threading block A

Threading block L | Threading block K | Threading block J | Threading block I | Threading block H | Threading block G

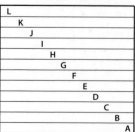

Threading profile draft

Warp 100-2 and 100-6 (adapted for loom-controlled weave)
(continued)

Threading repeat

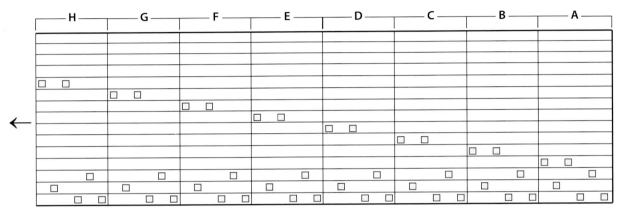

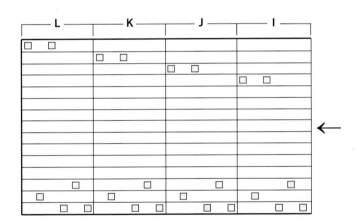

100-2

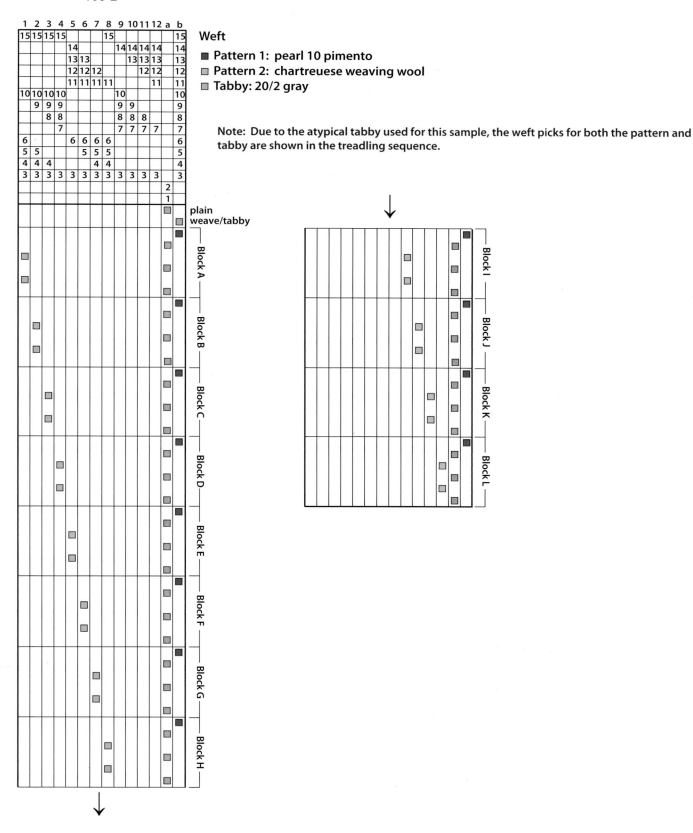

Weft

■ Pattern 1: pearl 10 pimento
□ Pattern 2: chartreuese weaving wool
□ Tabby: 20/2 gray

Note: Due to the atypical tabby used for this sample, the weft picks for both the pattern and tabby are shown in the treadling sequence.

100-6

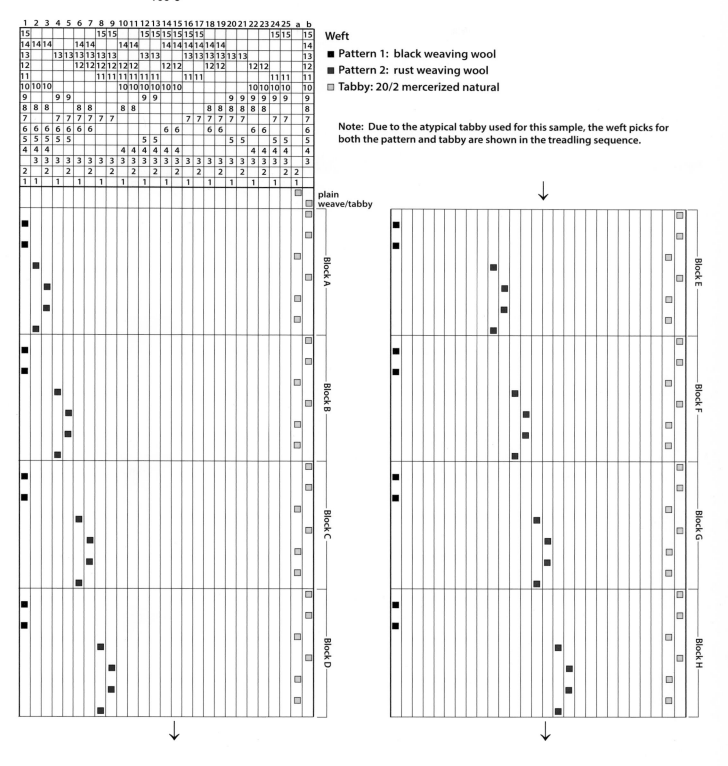

Weft

■ Pattern 1: black weaving wool

■ Pattern 2: rust weaving wool

□ Tabby: 20/2 mercerized natural

Note: Due to the atypical tabby used for this sample, the weft picks for both the pattern and tabby are shown in the treadling sequence.

100-6 (continued)

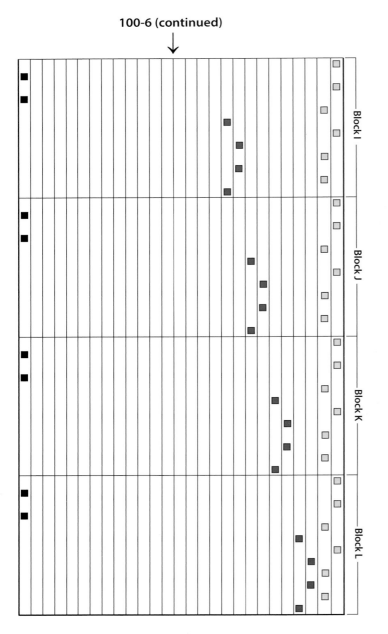

Block I

Block J

Block K

Block L

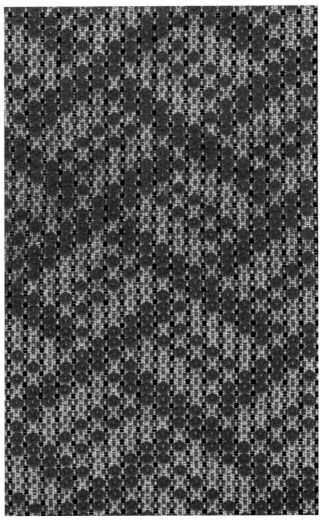

Multiple Tabby Weaves

The basic blocks developed by Dr. Bateman for the Multiple Tabby system are related to M's and O's. Like M's and O's, each block has a different pair of tabby shaft combinations treadled for the tabby. Blocks using four, six, and eight shafts were designed and used by Dr. Bateman. He developed other drafts by expanding and rearranging the threading within the original blocks. Some of Dr. Bateman's samples resemble M's and O's; however, most were treadled so there is no resemblance to the original inspiration weave.

Dr. Bateman chose to call these weaves Multiple Tabby because each block has a different tabby.

M&Os Threading Blocks

Threading block B

Threading block A

Original Multiple Tabby Threading Blocks

Block C   **Block B**   **Block A**

New blocks are created by rearranging the threading sequence

Block F   **Block E**   **Block D**

For more information about Multiple Tabby weaves, refer to Harvey, Virginia I., *Multiple Tabby Weaves, Based on Dr. William G. Bateman's Manuscript,* Shuttle Craft Guild Monograph 35 (Freeland, WA: HTH Publishers, 1981).

Warp 272A

Weave: Four-shaft Multiple Tabby
Sett: 30 epi
Warp: □ 20/2 natural cotton

Threading block F	Threading block E	Threading block D	Threading block C	Threading block B	Threading block A
4	4	4	4	4	4
3	3	3	3	3	3
2	2	2	2	2	2
1	1	1	1	1	1

Threading profile draft

F					
	E				
		D			
			C		
				B	
					A

Threading repeat

F ——— E ——— D ——— C ——— B ——— A

Note: Because of the threading sequence, a true plain weave for this threading is not possible.

272A - 6

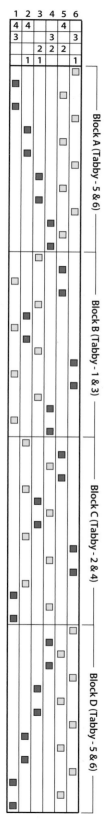

Weft

- ■ Pattern: Scarlet Fabri
- ☐ Tabby: pearl 20 linen color

Note: Due to the shift in the tabby treadles (hence, *multiple tabby*) the weft picks for both the pattern and tabby are shown in the treadling sequence. Also, because of the threading sequence, a true plain weave is not possible.

Warp 283

Weave: Four-shaft Multiple Tabby
Sett: 30 epi
Warp: ▣   20/2 deep coral

Threading block C

	4		4		4	
3		3		3		
			2		2	2
1					1	1

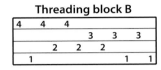

Threading block B

4		4		4		
				3	3	3
	2	2	2			
1					1	1

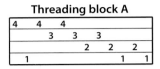

Threading block A

4		4		4		
		3	3	3		
			2	2	2	
1					1	1

Threading profile draft

C	
B	
	A

Threading repeat

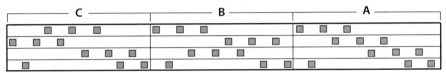

C ——————— B ——————— A

Note: Because of the threading sequence, a true plain
weave for this threading is not possible.

283 - 2

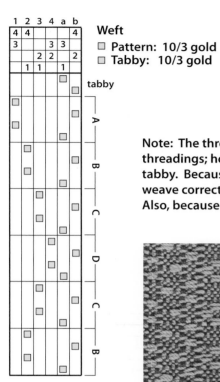

Weft
- ☐ Pattern: 10/3 gold
- ☐ Tabby: 10/3 gold

Treadling profile draft

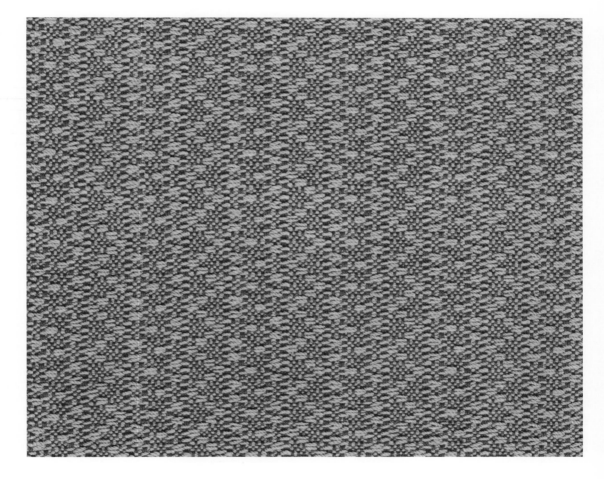

Note: The threading for this sample is one of Dr. Bateman's Multiple Tabby threadings; however, this particular sample is woven with a single alternating tabby. Because the order of the tabby picks is critical for the pattern to weave correctly, the tabby picks have been included in the treadling sequence. Also, because of the threading sequence, a true plain weave is not possible.

Extended Divided Twill Weaves

Dr. Bateman developed the Extended Divided Twill system by dividing an eight-shaft draft into two sections; the lower section with shafts one through four and the upper section with shafts five through eight. The threads are then alternatively placed in the two sections. In a simple divided twill, only one thread is placed in each section and they are threaded in a twill progression as shown below.

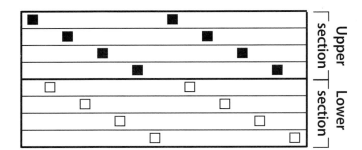

Dr. Bateman extended the divided twill by drafting one or more threads in the lower section before he placed a thread (or multiple threads) in the upper section or vice versa. The Extended Divided Twill is always drafted so the tabby picks may be woven by alternating the shafts odd-even. Blocks vary from three to eleven threads with straight twills, chevrons, and crackle units drafted as sections of the blocks.

As an example, below are the five-end threading blocks for the Bateman sample #274. For each block, there is a three-end chevron threaded in the lower section followed by a two-end straight draw threaded in the upper section.

Threading repeat

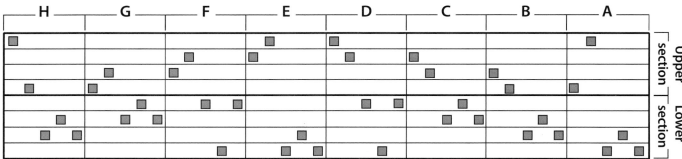

For more information about Extended Divided Twill weaves, refer to Harvey, Virginia I., *Extended Divided Twill Weaves, Based on Dr. William G. Bateman's Manuscript.* Shuttle Craft Guild Monograph 39, (Freeland, WA: HTH Publishers, 1988).

Warp 112

Weave: Eight-shaft Extended Divided Twill
Sett: 30 epi
Warp: □ 20/2 pearl ecru

Threading block D	Threading block C	Threading block B	Threading block A

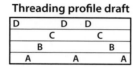

Threading profile draft

D		D	D
	C		C
B			B
A		A	A

Threading repeat

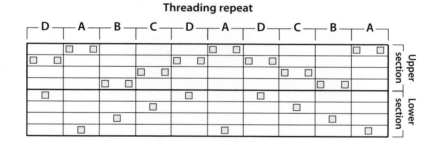

112-2

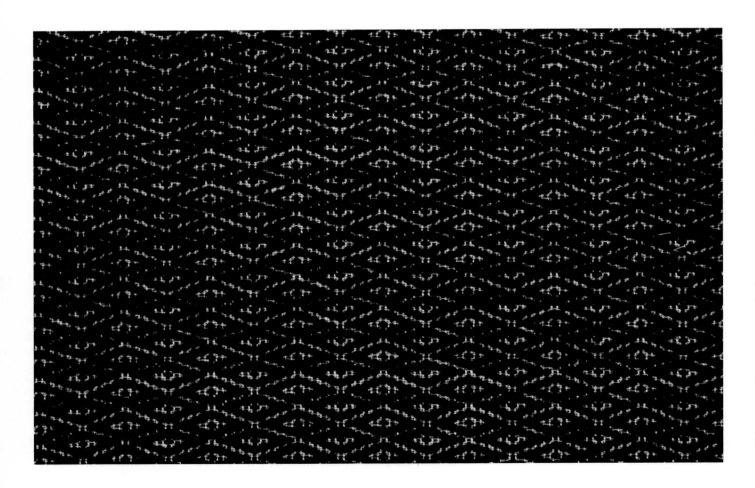

Weft

■ Pattern: silk navy blue floss

□ Tabby: 20/2 cotton dark ecru

□ plain weave/tabby

112-3

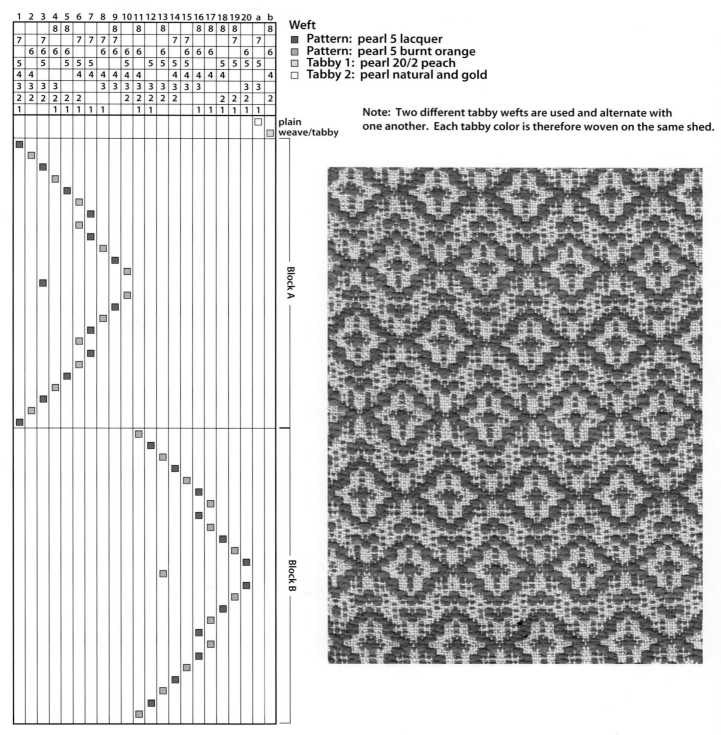

Weft
- ■ Pattern: pearl 5 lacquer
- ▦ Pattern: pearl 5 burnt orange
- ☐ Tabby 1: pearl 20/2 peach
- ☐ Tabby 2: pearl natural and gold

Note: Two different tabby wefts are used and alternate with one another. Each tabby color is therefore woven on the same shed.

Block A

Block B

Warp 113

Weave: Eight-shaft Extended Divided Twill
Sett: 30 epi
Warp: ☐ 20/2 natural mercerized cotton

Threading block D

7	
4	4

Threading block C

6	
3	3

Threading block B

5	
2	2

Threading block A

8	
1	1

Threading profile draft

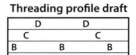

	D		D	
	C			C
B		B		B
	A	A		A

Threading repeat

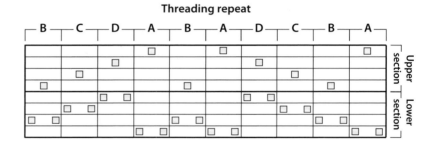

113-6

1	2	3	4	5	6	7	8	9	10	11	12	13	14	15	a	b
			8	8	8	8	8	8	8	8	8	8	8			8
7	7		7	7	7	7	7	7	7	7					7	
6	6	6	6	6	6		6				6	6	6	6		6
5	5	5	5			5	5	5		5	5	5	5	5		
	4	4	4	4	4	4	4			4						4
3	3	3	3			3						3	3	3		
	2								2	2	2	2	2	2		2
				1	1	1	1	1	1	1			1	1		

plain weave/tabby

Weft
☐ Pattern1 : pearl 5 topaz
▨ Pattern 2: pearl 5 beaver
◼ Pattern 3: pearl 5 light rust
■ Pattern 4: pearl 5 mahogany
☐ Tabby: 20/2 natural mercerized cotton

Note: Four pattern colors rotate in this sample. The rotation of the colors is mirrored in the second half, except for the pattern picks where the treadling sequence pivots.

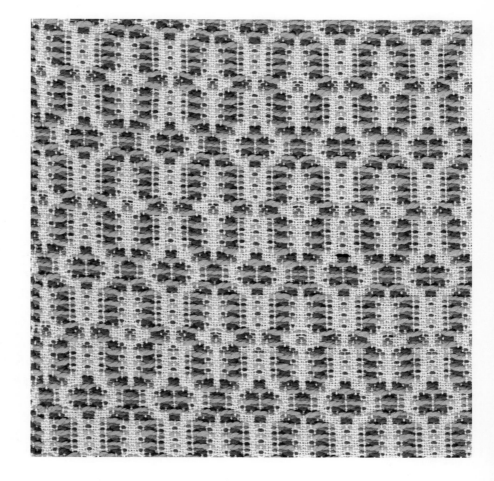

113-8

Weft

- ■ Pattern 1: pearl 5 raspberry
- ■ Pattern 2: pearl 5 cranapple
- □ Tabby: natural and gold

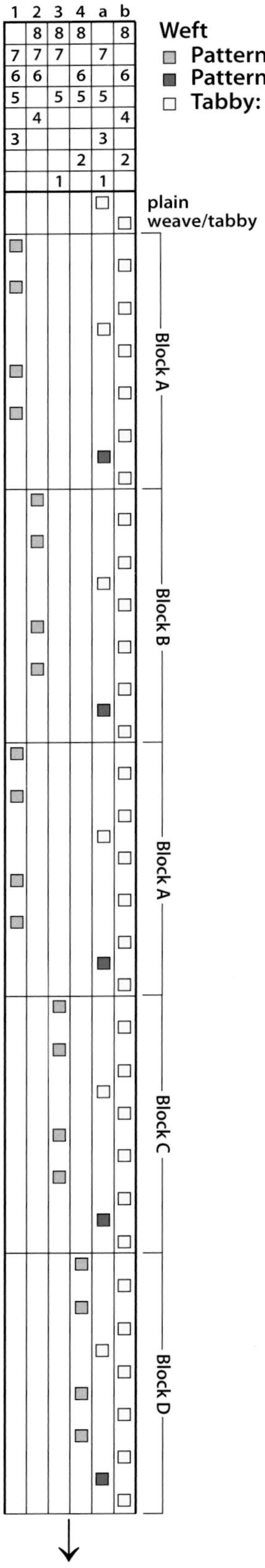

Treadling profile draft

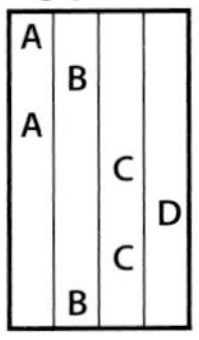

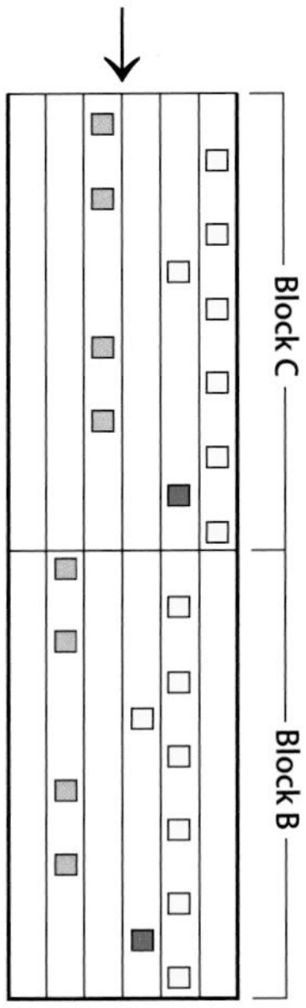

Note: Due to the atypical tabby used for this sample, the weft picks for both the pattern and tabby are shown in the treadling sequence.

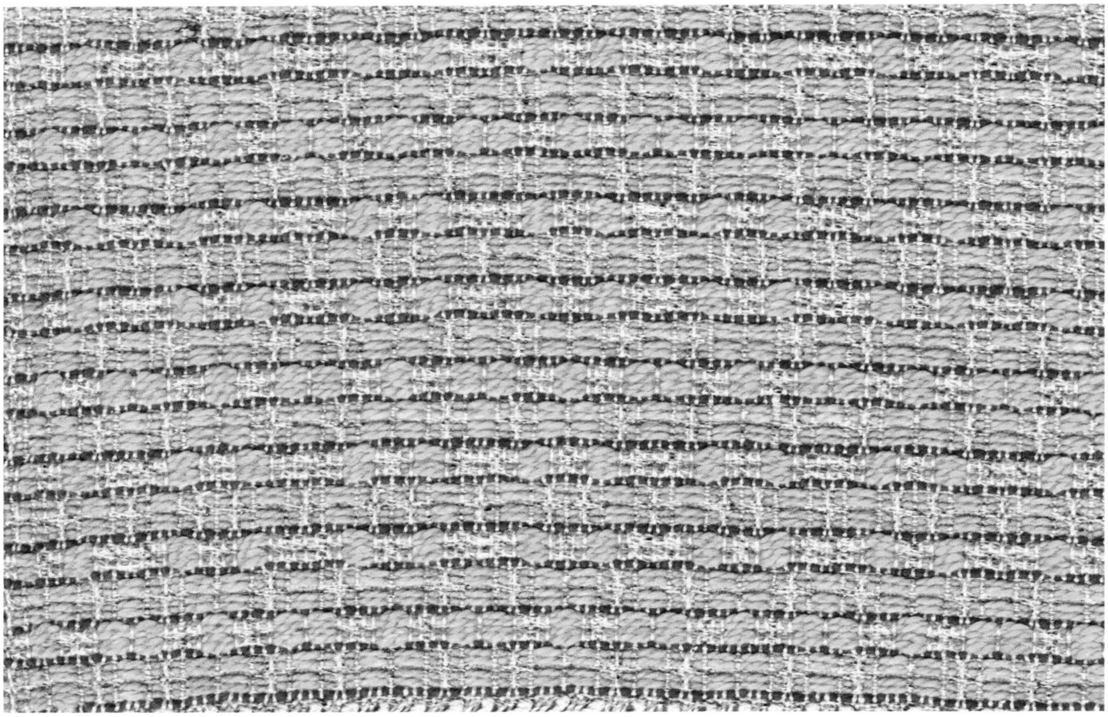

plain weave/tabby

Block A

Block B

Block A

Block C

Block D

Block C

Block B

Warp 115

Weave: Eight-shaft Extended Divided Twill

Sett: 30 epi

Warp 1: ■ 20/2 pearl cotton burnt orange (warp ends on shafts 5-6-7-8)

Warp 2: ■ 20/2 pearl cotton lavender (warp ends on shaft 1)

Warp 3: □ 20/2 pearl cotton natural (warp ends on shaft 2)

Warp 4: ■ 20/2 pearl cotton linen (warp ends on shaft 3)

Warp 5: ■ 20/2 pearl cotton raspberry (warp ends on shaft 4)

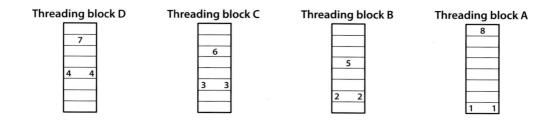

Threading block D   Threading block C   Threading block B   Threading block A

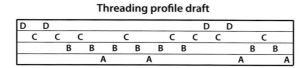

Threading profile draft

Threading repeat

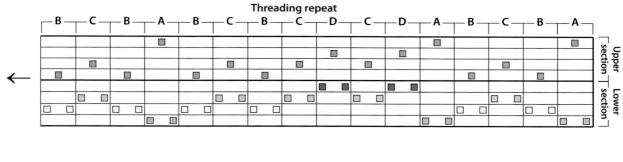

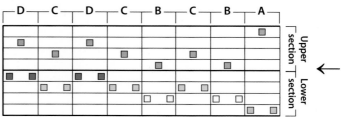

115-3

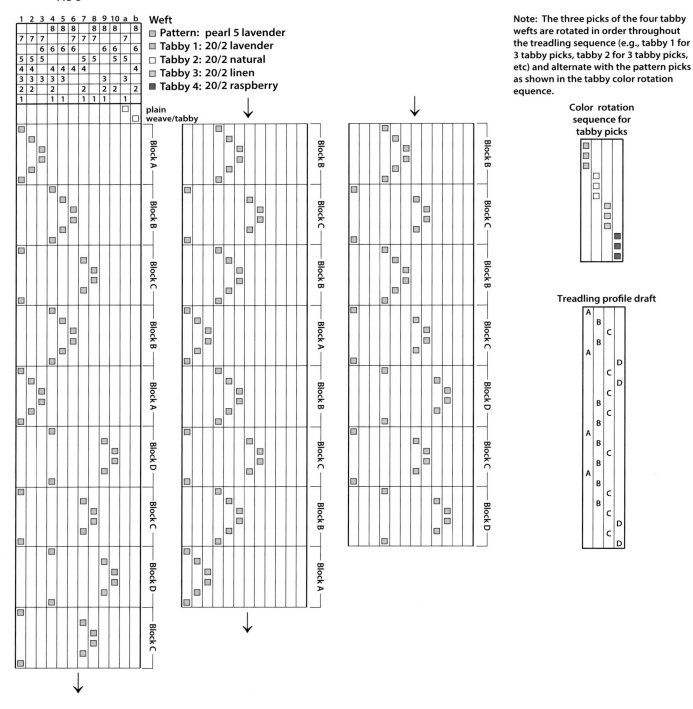

Weft
- ☐ Pattern: pearl 5 lavender
- ☐ Tabby 1: 20/2 lavender
- ☐ Tabby 2: 20/2 natural
- ☐ Tabby 3: 20/2 linen
- ■ Tabby 4: 20/2 raspberry

plain weave/tabby

Note: The three picks of the four tabby wefts are rotated in order throughout the treadling sequence (e.g., tabby 1 for 3 tabby picks, tabby 2 for 3 tabby picks, etc) and alternate with the pattern picks as shown in the tabby color rotation equence.

Color rotation sequence for tabby picks

Treadling profile draft

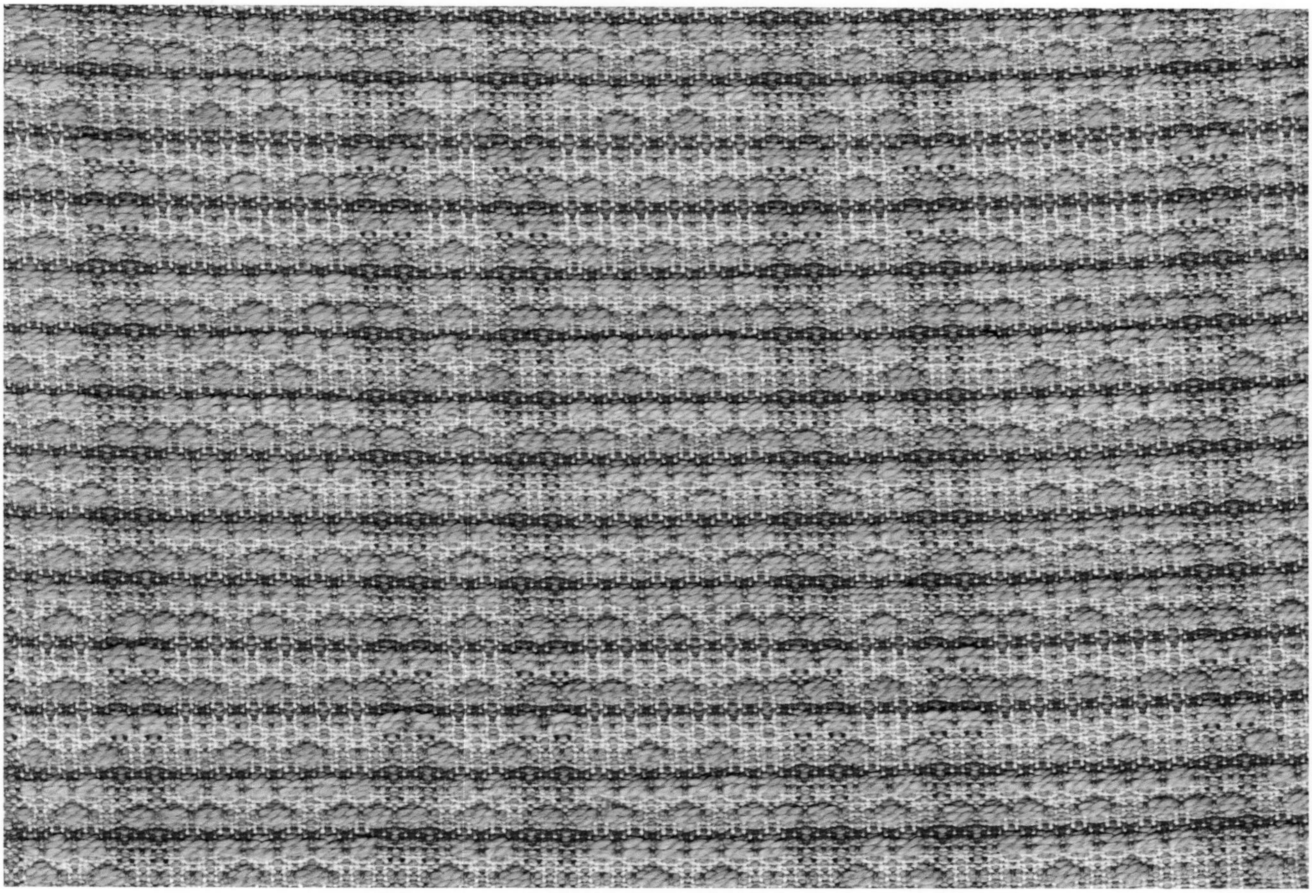

115-5

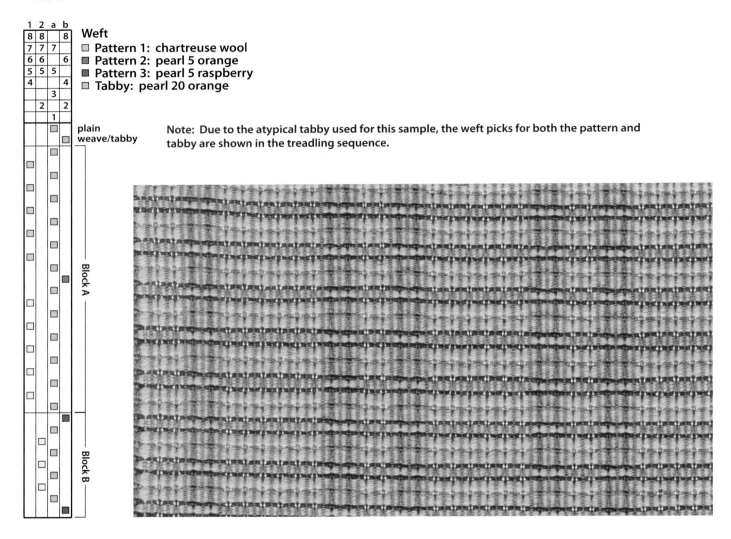

Weft
☐ Pattern 1: chartreuse wool
■ Pattern 2: pearl 5 orange
■ Pattern 3: pearl 5 raspberry
☐ Tabby: pearl 20 orange

Note: Due to the atypical tabby used for this sample, the weft picks for both the pattern and tabby are shown in the treadling sequence.

115-8

	1	2	3	4	5	6	7	8	9	10	a	b
		8		8	8			8		8		8
	7		7		7		7		7		7	
		6		6		6		6	6			6
	5		5		5		5		5		5	
	4		4			4	4			4		4
		3		3		3	3		3		3	
	2		2			2	2			2		2
		1	1		1			1	1		1	1

plain weave/tabby

Block A

Block B

Weft

- ☐ Pattern 1: lavender
- ☐ Pattern 2: "opposite" pattern - deep rose
- ☐ Tabby: deep rose

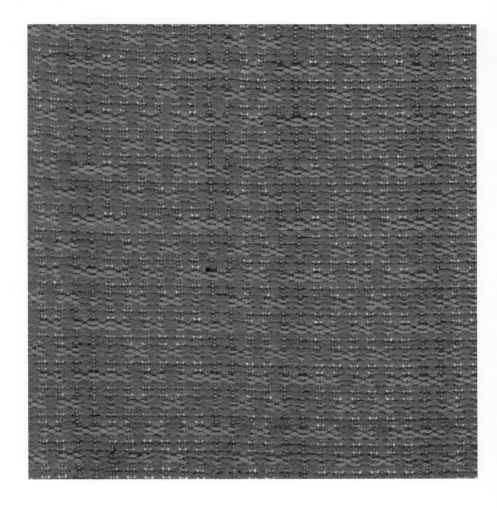

Warp 117

Weave: Eight-shaft Extended Divided Twill

Sett: 30 epi

Block A: ▣ 20/2 coral (except pearl 5 ☐ buff warp end on shaft 2)

Block B: ☐ 20/2 buff (except pearl 5 ☐ yellow warp end on shaft 3)

Block C: ☐ 20/2 yellow (except pearl 5 ▣ chartreuse warp end on shaft 4)

Block D: ▣ 20/2 chartreuse (except pearl 5 ▣ crabapple warp end on shaft 1)

Threading block D	Threading block C	Threading block B	Threading block A

Threading profile draft

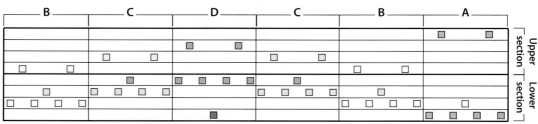

Threading repeat

117-3

	1	2	3	4	5	6
	8					8
				7	7	
			6			6
		5			5	
	4	4	4			4
	3	3		3	3	
	2		2	2		2
		1	1	1	1	

□ plain
□ weave

Block A
Block B
Block C
Block D

Weft
■ Pattern 1: pearl 20 peacock blue
■ Pattern 2: pearl 3 rust

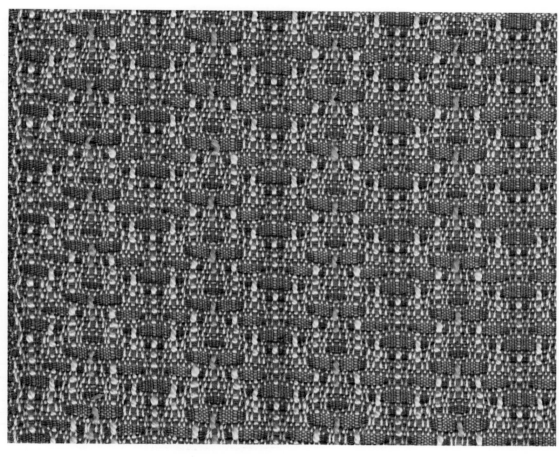

117-6

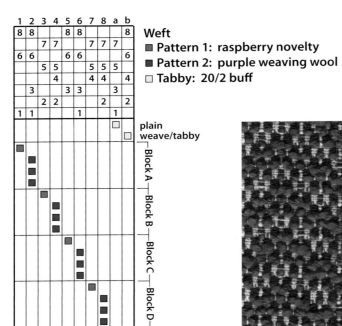

Weft
- ■ Pattern 1: raspberry novelty
- ■ Pattern 2: purple weaving wool
- □ Tabby: 20/2 buff

Warp 122

Weave: Eight-shaft Extended Divided Twill
Sett: 30 epi
Warp: ☐ pearl 20 ecru

Threading block D	Threading block C	Threading block B	Threading block A

The threading for warp #122 is based on the above four threading blocks. In the threading repeat below, these four blocks have been manipulated by reversing the sequences and including transition ends. This allows the blocks to be used in different ways; however, it prohibits the ability to produce a threading profile draft.

The first half of the threading sequence, shown in the upper portion of the illustration below, is repeated in a reverse sequence after the pivot point and shown in the lower portion.

Threading repeat

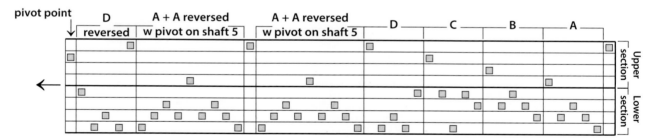

122-7

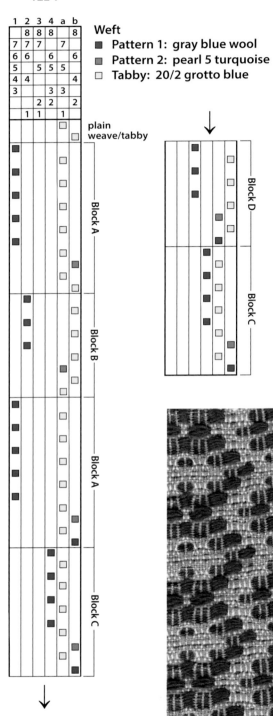

Weft

■ Pattern 1: gray blue wool
■ Pattern 2: pearl 5 turquoise
□ Tabby: 20/2 grotto blue

plain weave/tabby

Block A
Block B
Block A
Block C

Treadling profile draft

Block D
Block C

Note: Due to the atypical tabby used for this sample (e.g., all tabby picks are done on the same treadle), the weft picks for both the pattern and tabby are shown in the treadling sequence.

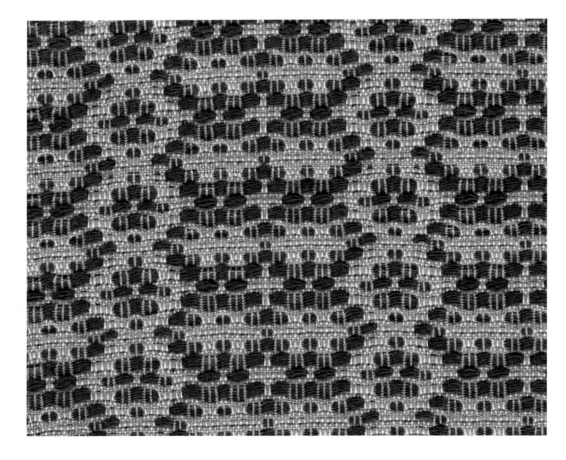

Warp 135

Weave: Eight-shaft Extended Divided Twill
Sett: 30 epi
Warp 1: ■ 20/2 dark blue (shafts 1, 2, 3, and 4)
Warp 2: □ 20/2 light blue (outside ends on shafts 5, 6, 7, and 8)
Warp 3: □ 10/3 light gray (center end on shafts 5, 6, 7, and 8)

Threading block D	Threading block C	Threading block B	Threading block A

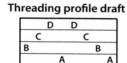

Threading profile draft

Threading repeat

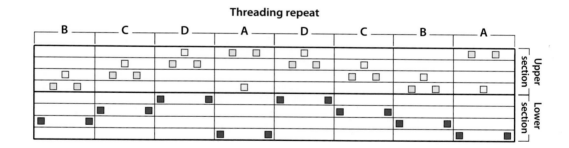

135-5

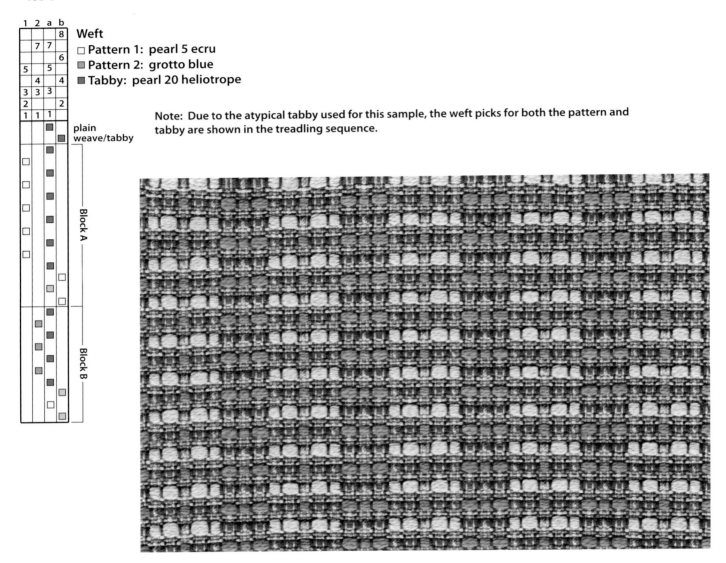

Weft
☐ Pattern 1: pearl 5 ecru
▪ Pattern 2: grotto blue
▪ Tabby: pearl 20 heliotrope

Note: Due to the atypical tabby used for this sample, the weft picks for both the pattern and tabby are shown in the treadling sequence.

Warp 167

Weave: Eight-shaft Extended Divided Twill
Sett: 30 epi
Warp: ◧ Bernat Umbrian gold

Threading block D   Threading block C   Threading block B   Threading block A

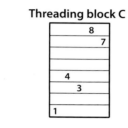
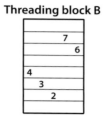
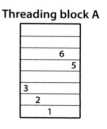

Threading profile draft

Threading repeat

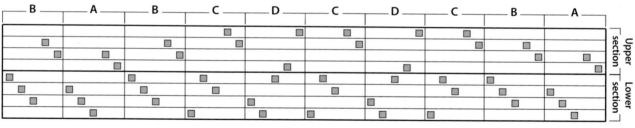

167-4

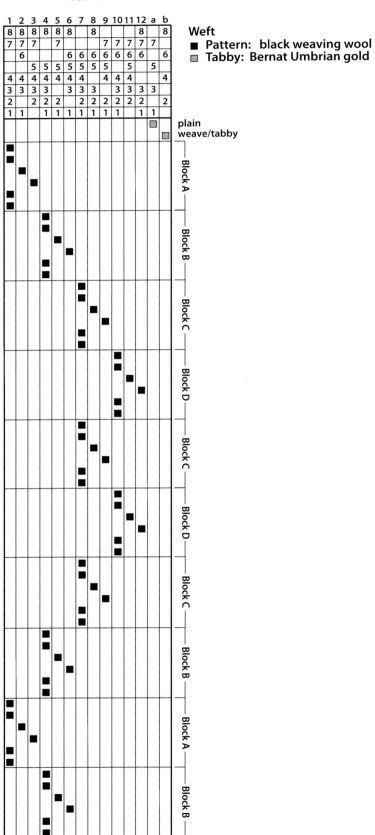

Weft

■ Pattern: black weaving wool
▨ Tabby: Bernat Umbrian gold

plain weave/tabby

Treadling profile draft

167-7

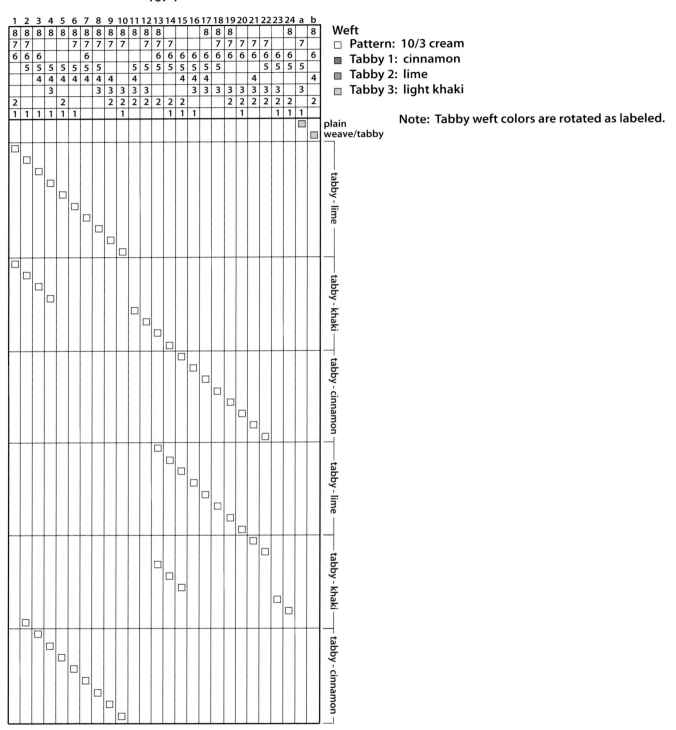

Weft

☐ Pattern: 10/3 cream
◼ Tabby 1: cinnamon
◼ Tabby 2: lime
◻ Tabby 3: light khaki

Note: Tabby weft colors are rotated as labeled.

Warp 175

Weave: Eight-shaft Extended Divided Twill
Sett: 30 epi
Warp: ■ Swedish cotton, medium heliotrope

Threading block D   **Threading block C**   **Threading block B**   **Threading block A**

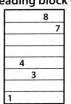

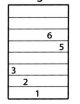

Threading block H   **Threading block G**   **Threading block F**   **Threading block E**

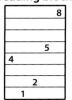
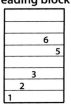

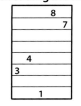

Threading profile draft

		H			
			G		
	F			F	
		E			E
D					D
	C				C
		B			B
		A			A

Threading repeat

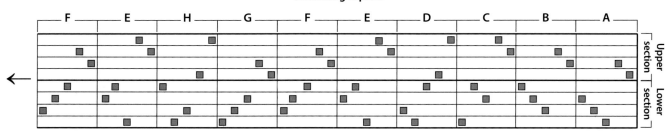

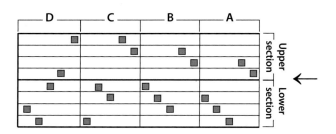

175-2

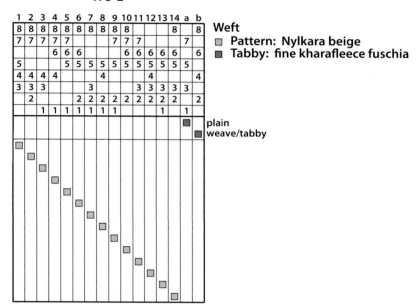

1	2	3	4	5	6	7	8	9	10	11	12	13	14	a	b
8	8	8	8	8	8	8	8	8						8	8
7	7	7	7						7	7	7			7	
			6	6	6				6	6	6	6	6		6
5			5	5	5	5	5	5	5	5	5	5	5		
4	4	4				4			4					4	
3	3	3			3				3	3	3	3	3		
	2			2	2	2	2	2	2	2	2			2	
	1	1	1	1	1	1	1					1		1	

Weft

☐ **Pattern: Nylkara beige**

■ **Tabby: fine kharafleece fuschia**

■ plain
■ weave/tabby

175-4 (part 1)

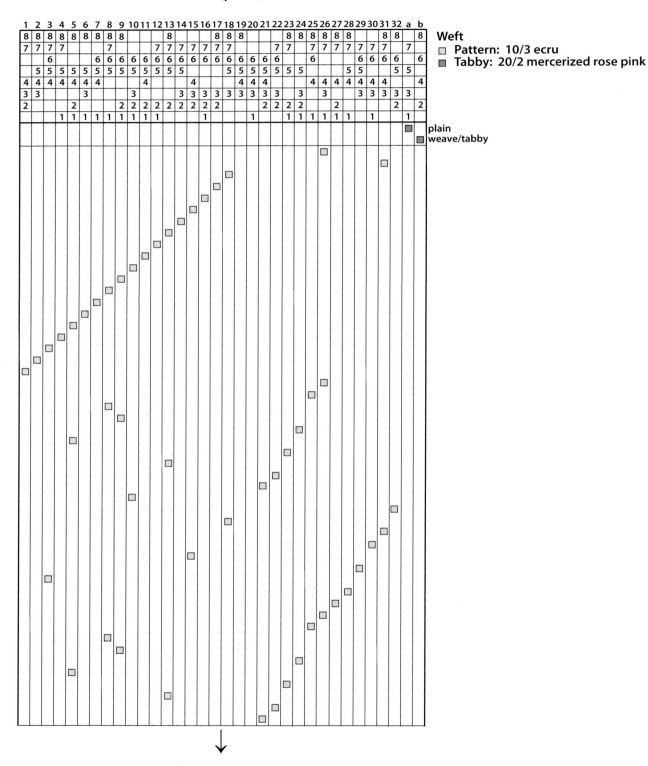

Weft

☐ Pattern: 10/3 ecru

▨ Tabby: 20/2 mercerized rose pink

plain
weave/tabby

175-4 (part 2)

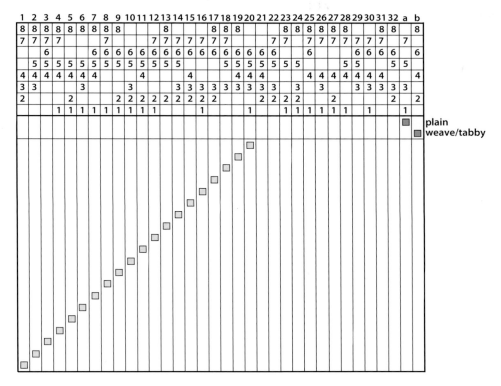

plain weave/tabby

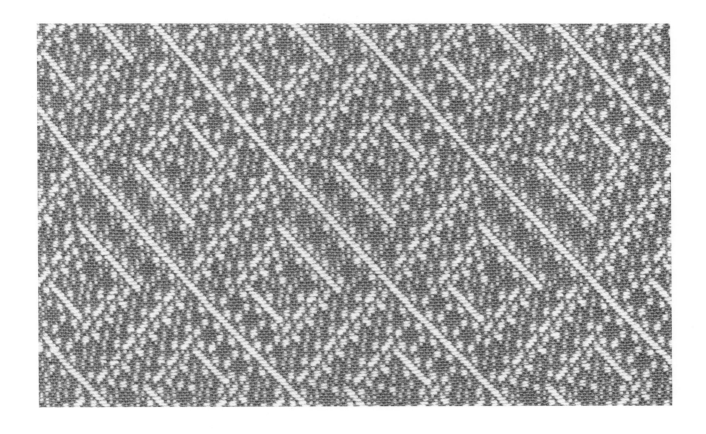

175-6

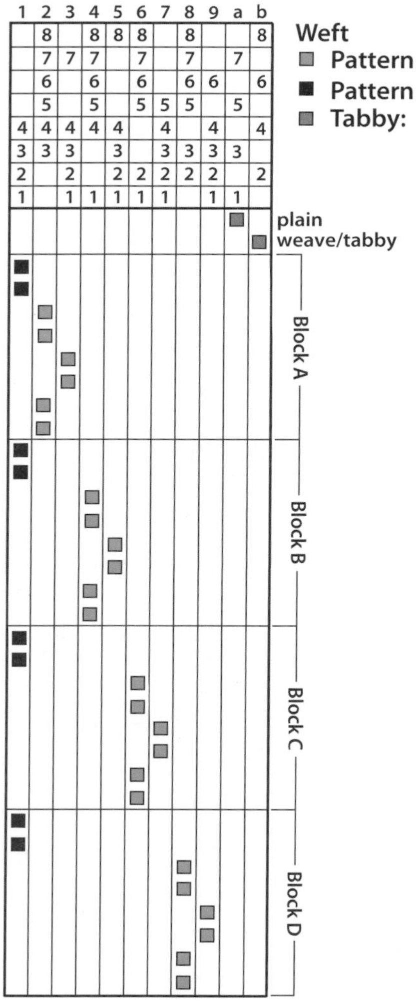

Weft

- ▪ Pattern 1: weaving wool aqua
- ▪ Pattern 2: pearl 5 black
- ▪ Tabby: 20/2 mercerized lavender

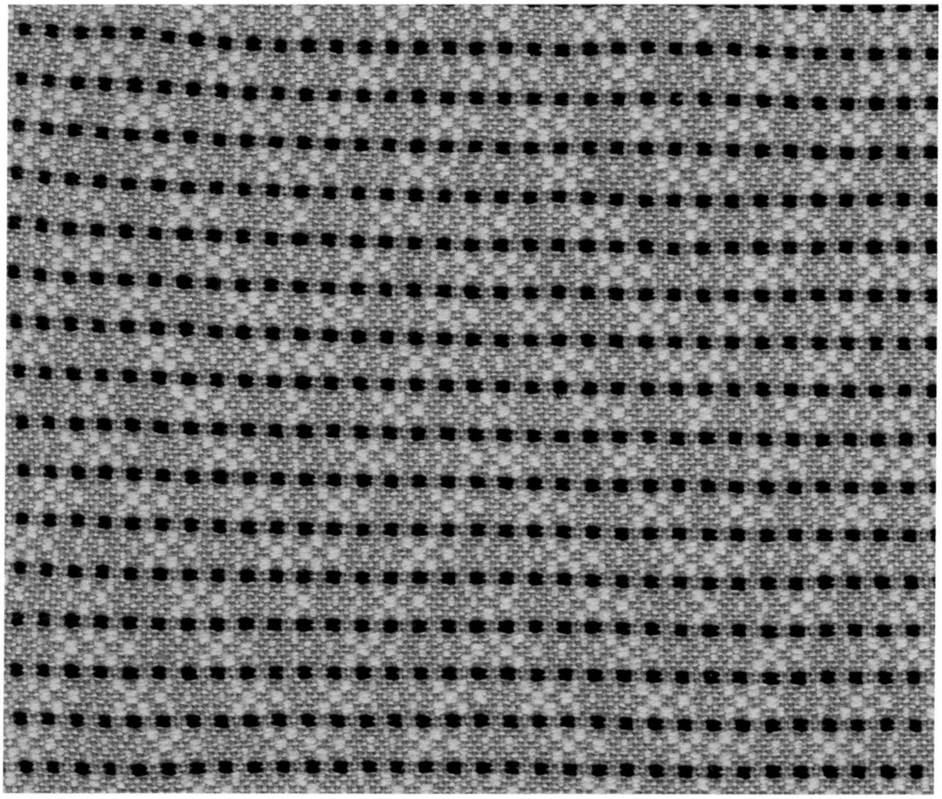

175-8

1	2	3	4	a	b
8	8	8			8
7	7		7	7	
6		6	6		6
	5	5	5	5	
4					4
		3	3		
	2				2
1			1		

plain
weave/tabby

Block A
tabby - heliotrope

Block B
tabby - rose

Weft

■ Pattern 1: orange floss
■ Tabby 1: Swedish cotton medium heliotrope
■ Tabby 2: Swedish cotton rose

Warp 274

Weave: Eight-shaft Extended Divided Twill
Sett: 30 epi
Warp: ■ pearl 20 cork

Threading block D

8	
7	
4	4
1	

Threading block C

7	
6	
4	
3	3

Threading block B

6	
5	
3	
2	2

Threading block A

8	
5	
2	
1	1

Threading block H

8	
5	
3	
2	2

Threading block G

6	
5	
4	
3	3

Threading block F

7	
6	
4	4
1	

Threading block E

8	
7	
2	
1	1

Threading profile draft

H							
	G						
		F					
			E				
				D			
					C		
						B	
							A

Threading repeat

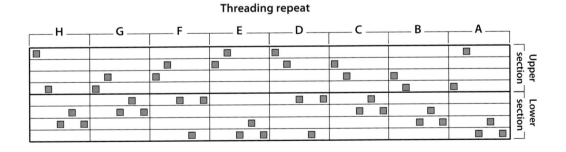

274-6

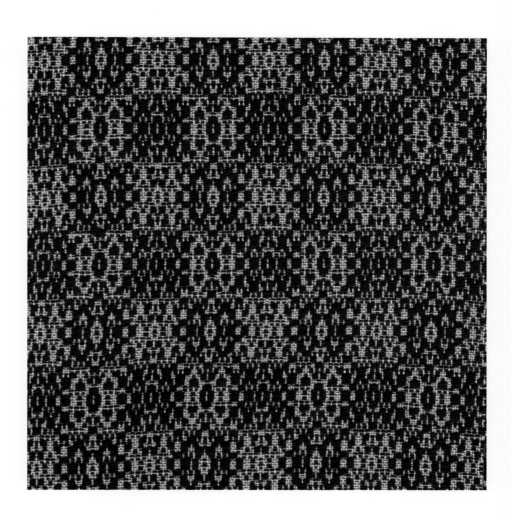

Weft
- Pattern: 10/3 wine
- Tabby: pearl 20 cork

plain weave/tabby

Block A

Block B

Extended Manifold Twill Weaves

A manifold twill is a sequence created from more than one twill sequence. In the example below, it is developed by placing a twill threading sequence on shaft 1 and another twill threading sequence that begins on any other shaft except 2. Both threads begin a straight twill that extends through a given number of shafts and then a repeat begins. Below is an example of a manifold twill with an eight-shaft straight draw twill with the first thread on shaft one alternating with an eight-shaft straight draw twill that begins on shaft five. Unlike the Extended Divided Twill, there is no lower or upper section.

Dr. Bateman extended Manifold Twills by adding one or more threads on adjacent shafts to one or both of the original threads. The sequences create twills, chevrons, crackle groups, or other arrangements that are drafted so they have tabby picks woven odd-even.

Dr. Bateman stated that Extended Manifold Twills were related to the Extended Divided Twills. Extended Manifold Twills are based on manifold twill drafts which resemble divided twill drafts except that they have more than two lines of threads within a draft.

For more information about Extended Manifold Twill weaves, refer to Harvey, Virginia I., *Extended Divided Twill Weaves, Based on Dr. William G. Bateman's Manuscript*, Shuttle Craft Guild Monograph 40 (Freeland, WA: HTH Publishers, 1989).

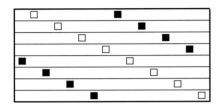

Warp 120

Weave: Eight-shaft Extended Manifold Twill
Sett: 22½ epi
Warp 1: ☐ 10/3 cotton lemon tint
Warp 2: ■ pearl 10 pimento

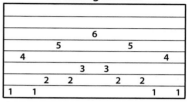

Threading block B

8		8					8		8
	7		7			2		2	
		6		6					
5							5		
		4			4				
			3						

Threading block A

				6					
			5			5			
4								4	
		3		3					
	2		2		2		2		
1		1					1		1

Threading profile draft

Threading repeat

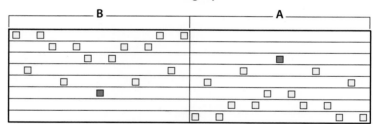

120-2

1	2	3	4	5	6	a	b
	8			8	8	8		8
	7	7	7			7		
6				6	6			6
		5		5	5	5		
	4	4			4			4
3	3		3			3		
2				2	2			2
1	1	1		1		1		

Weft
- ☐ Pattern 1: 10/3 cotton lemon tint
- ■ Pattern 2: pearl 10 pimento
- ■ Pattern 3: olive rayon novelty
- ◻ Tabby: #50 medium olive mercerized

plain weave/tabby

Block A

Block B

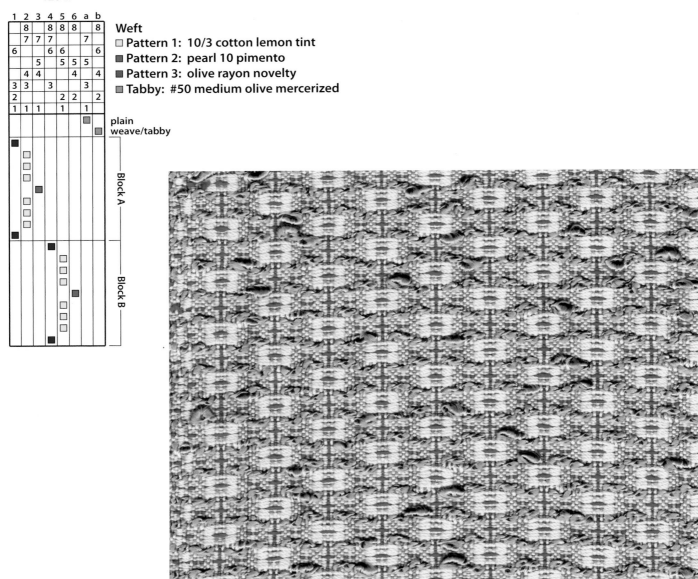

120-7

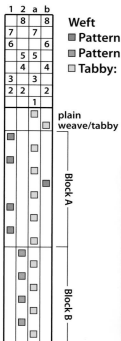

Weft
- ■ Pattern 1: pearl 3 jade
- ■ Pattern 2: grotto blue
- □ Tabby: Beauty Glo chartreuse and gold

Note: Due to the atypical tabby used for this sample, the weft picks for both the pattern and tabby are shown in the treadling sequence.

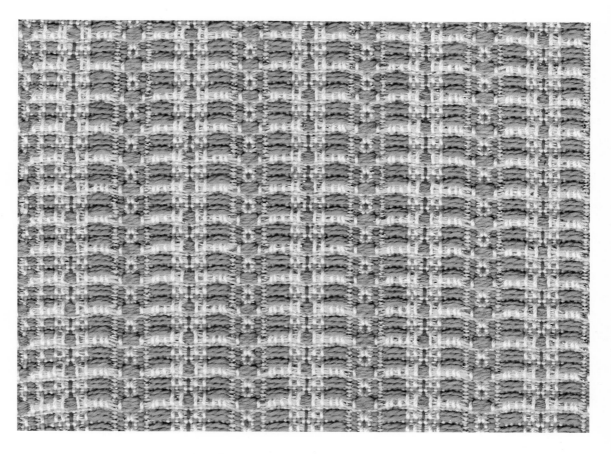

Warp 205

Weave: Eight-shaft Extended Manifold Twill
Sett: 37½ epi
Warp: ■ Star aptex gray

Threading block D

Threading block C

Threading block B

Threading block A

Threading block H

Threading block G

Threading block F

Threading block E

Threading profile draft

H				H		H	
G		G	
	F		F	
	E		E	
	D		D	
	C		C	
	B		B	
A		A		A

Threading repeat

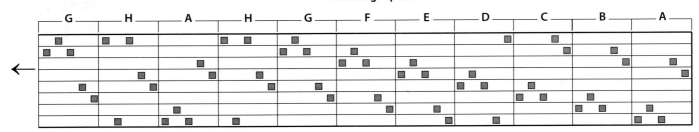

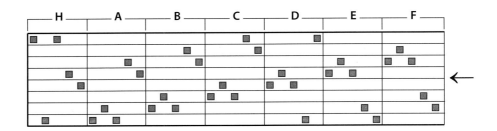

205-2

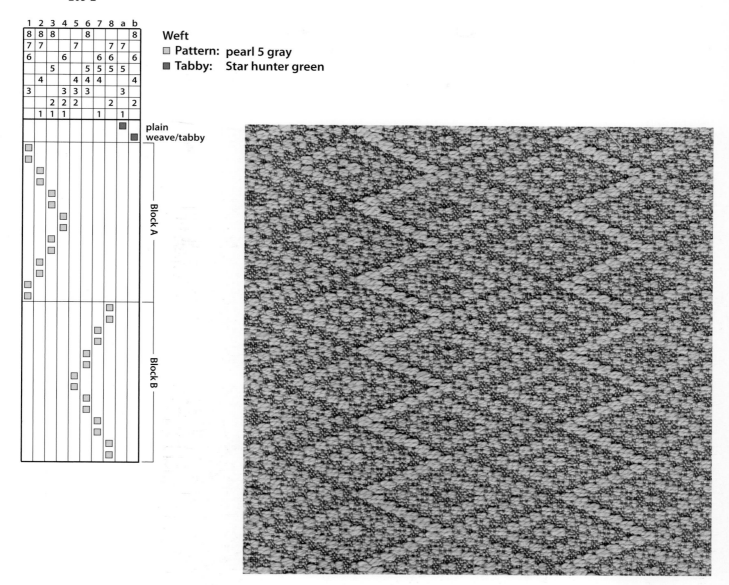

1	2	3	4	5	6	7	8	a	b
8	8	8			8				8
7	7			7				7	7
6			6			6	6		6
		5			5	5	5	5	
	4			4	4	4			4
3			3	3	3			3	
		2	2	2				2	2
	1	1	1				1		1

plain weave/tabby

Block A

Block B

Weft
- ☐ Pattern: pearl 5 gray
- ■ Tabby: Star hunter green

205-4

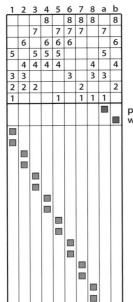

Weft
- ■ Pattern: 10/3 burnt orange
- ■ Tabby: Star copper brown

plain
weave/tabby

205-5

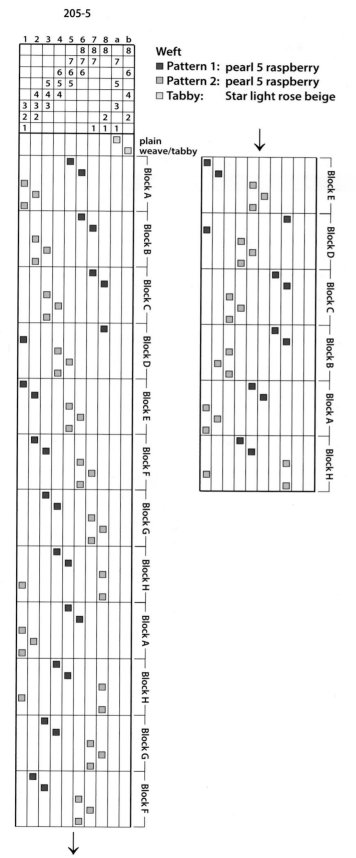

Weft
- ■ Pattern 1: pearl 5 raspberry
- ◼ Pattern 2: pearl 5 raspberry
- ☐ Tabby: Star light rose beige

Treadling profile draft

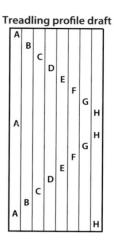

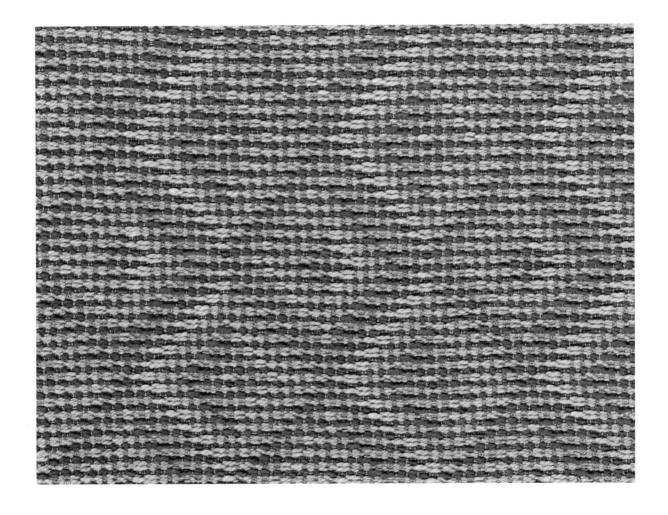

205-6

Weft
☐ **Pattern:** pearl 5 gray
■ **Tabby:** Star hunter green

plain weave/tabby

Block A

Block B

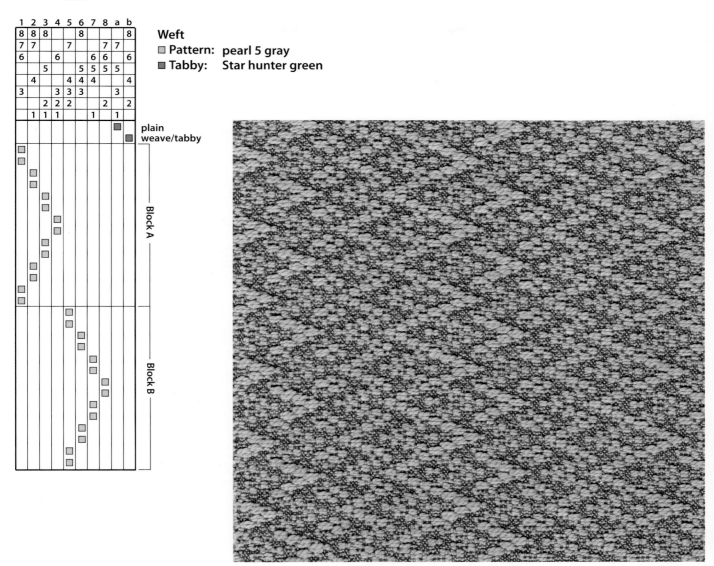

205-7

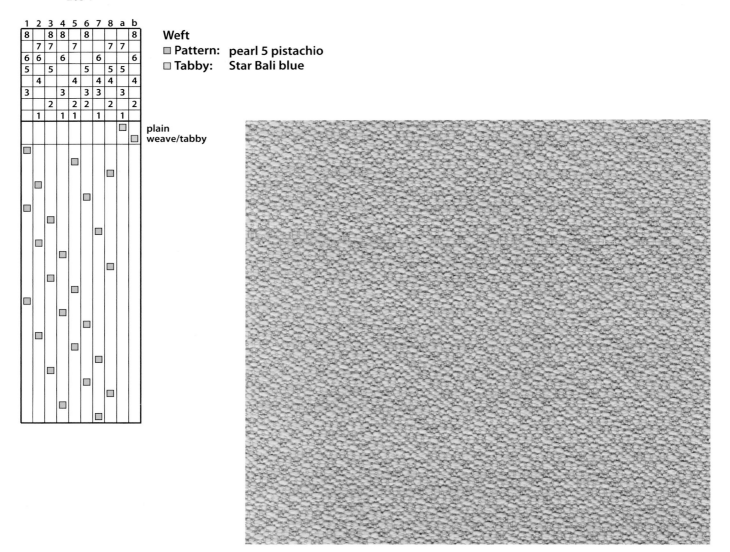

Weft
- **Pattern:** pearl 5 pistachio
- **Tabby:** Star Bali blue

205-9

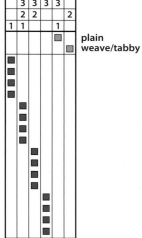

Weft
- ■ **Pattern:** dark green-ish blue wool
- ■ **Tabby:** Star aptex gray

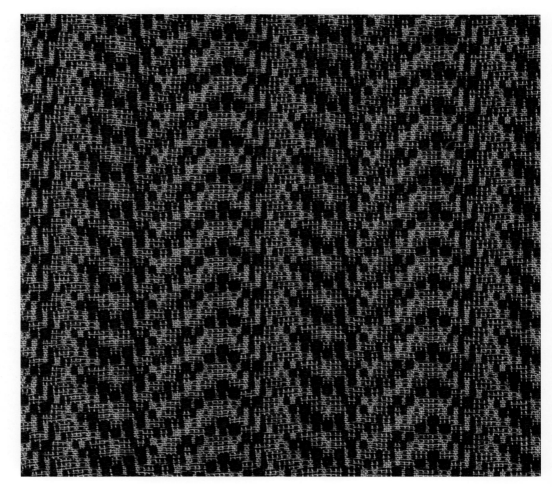

205-11

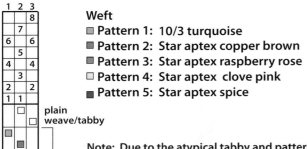

Weft
- Pattern 1: 10/3 turquoise
- Pattern 2: Star aptex copper brown
- Pattern 3: Star aptex raspberry rose
- Pattern 4: Star aptex clove pink
- Pattern 5: Star aptex spice

Note: Due to the atypical tabby and pattern weft changes used for this sample, the weft picks for both the pattern and tabby are shown in the treadling sequence.

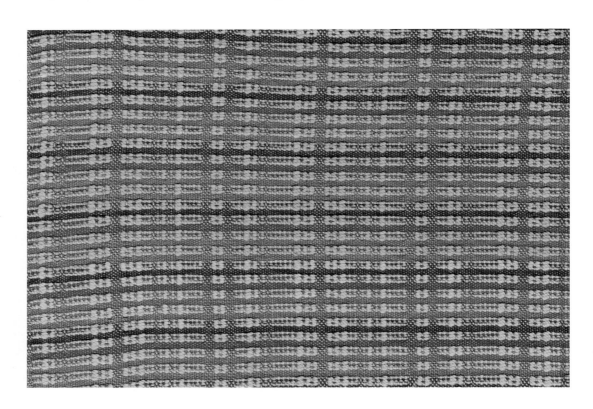

Warp 330

Weave: Eight-shaft Extended Manifold Twill
Sett: 30 epi
Warp: ▪ Star aptex gray

Threading block D

8		8
	6	
		5
4		4
1		

Threading block C

	8	
7		7
	4	
		4
		3
1		

Threading block B

	7	
6		6
4		
		3
		2
1		

Threading block A

	8	
	6	
5		5
3		
		2
		1

Threading block H

		8
7		
	5	
4		4
	2	
		1

Threading block G

		8
		7
	6	
	4	
3		3
	1	

Threading block F

	8	
		7
		6
	5	
	3	
2		2

Threading block E

	7	
		6
		5
4		
	2	
1		1

Threading profile draft

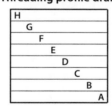

Threading repeat

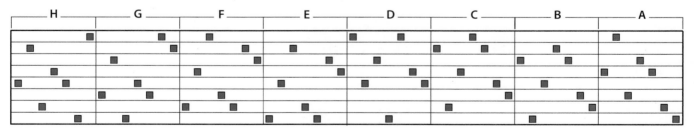

330-4

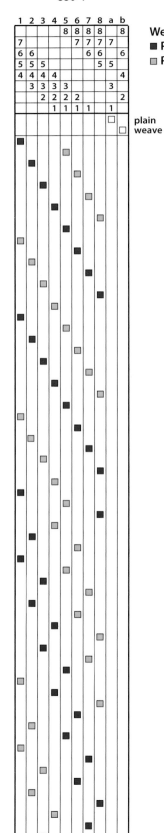

	1	2	3	4	5	6	7	8	a	b
					8	8	8	8		8
7	7					7	7	7	7	
6	6	6					6	6		6
5	5	5	5					5	5	
4	4	4	4	4						4
3		3	3	3	3				3	
2			2	2	2	2				2
1				1	1	1	1		1	

Weft

■ **Pattern 1: 10/3 dark green**
□ **Pattern 2: 10/3 lily green**

□ plain
□ weave

Park, Boulevard, and Chevron Weaves

Park weave

Park, Boulevard, and Chevron weaves are closely related. Each has a tie unit and a pattern unit. The Park weave has a one-end tie unit. The Boulevard weave has a three-end tie unit. The Chevron weave has a five-end tie portion of the unit. Some of the pattern units of these three weaves are interchangeable. For all three of these weaves, blocks with more ends and/or more shafts are possible. Also, the tabby weft picks are woven by alternating the odd-even shafts.

Park weave blocks consist of one tie end and pattern ends. The tie portion of the unit is one thread on shaft 1 at the beginning of the block. The remaining threads in the block are the pattern threads and consist of an odd number of threads (e.g., 3, 5, 7) which begin and end on the same even-numbered shaft. The pattern threads create a symmetrical 3-end chevron form. All of Dr. Bateman's Park weaves are threaded on seven or eight shafts and the blocks vary from four to fourteen threads.

Examples of Park weave blocks

Threading block C   **Threading block B**   **Threading block A**

Boulevard weave

The Boulevard weave is the same as the Park weave except the block has three tie ends, which are threaded 1-2-1. The pattern ends and tabby picks are managed the same way as in Park weaves, except shaft two may not be used for pattern ends. Six-thread, eight-thread, ten-thread, and twelve-thread blocks were drafted by Dr. Bateman.

Examples of Boulevard weave blocks

Threading block C   **Threading block B**   **Threading block A**

Chevron weave

The Chevron weave is an extension of the Boulevard weave. Shaft three is added to the tie sequence making it a five-end chevron threaded 1-2-3-2-1. The pattern ends in the block are the same as the Park and Boulevard weaves, except the number of ends is limited because there are three shafts required for the tie ends. Dr. Bateman drafted eight-shaft blocks with ten, twelve, fourteen, sixteen, and twenty threads.

Examples of Chevron weave blocks

Threading block C

	7				
6		6			
5			5		
4				4	
					3
			2	2	
					1	1

Threading block B

8		8			
7			7		
6				6	
	5				
				3	
		2	2		
1					1

Threading block A

8				8	
	7				
6	6				
5		5			
				3	
		2	2		
1					1

For more information about Park weaves, refer to Harvey, Virginia I., *Park Weaves, Based on Dr. William G. Bateman's Manuscript*, Shuttle Craft Guild Monograph 37 (Freeland, WA: HTH Publishers, 1984).

For more information about Boulevard and Chevron weaves, refer to Harvey, Virginia I., *Boulevard, Chevron, and Combination Weaves, Based on Dr. William G. Bateman's Manuscript*, Shuttle Craft Guild Monograph 38 (Freeland, WA: HTH Publishers, 1987).

Warp 302

Weave: Four-shaft Park
Sett: 30 epi
Warp: pearl 20 nutaupe

Threading block B   **Threading block A**

Threading profile draft

Threading repeat

302-1

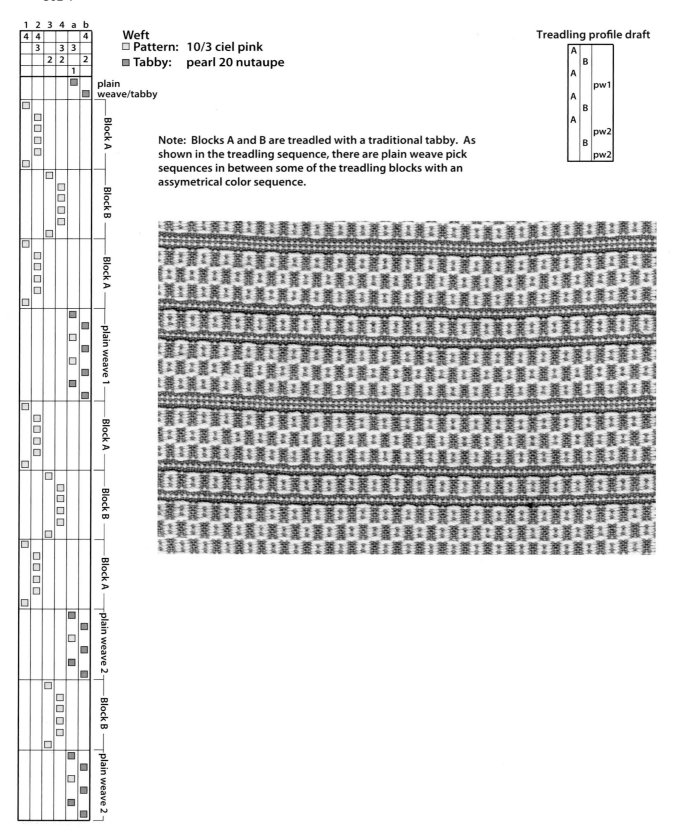

Weft
- ☐ **Pattern:** 10/3 ciel pink
- ◼ **Tabby:** pearl 20 nutaupe

Treadling profile draft

Note: Blocks A and B are treadled with a traditional tabby. As shown in the treadling sequence, there are plain weave pick sequences in between some of the treadling blocks with an assymetrical color sequence.

302-2

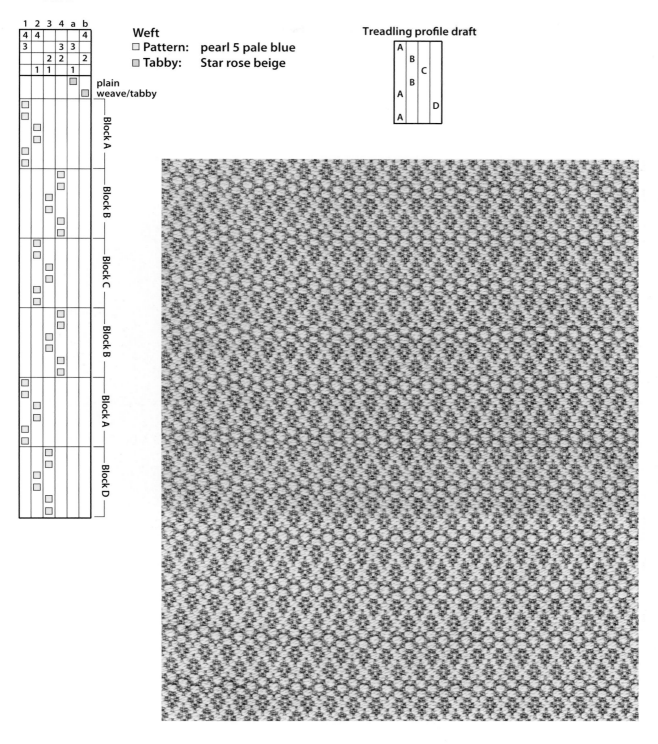

Weft
- ☐ **Pattern:** pearl 5 pale blue
- ☐ **Tabby:** Star rose beige

Treadling profile draft

302-3

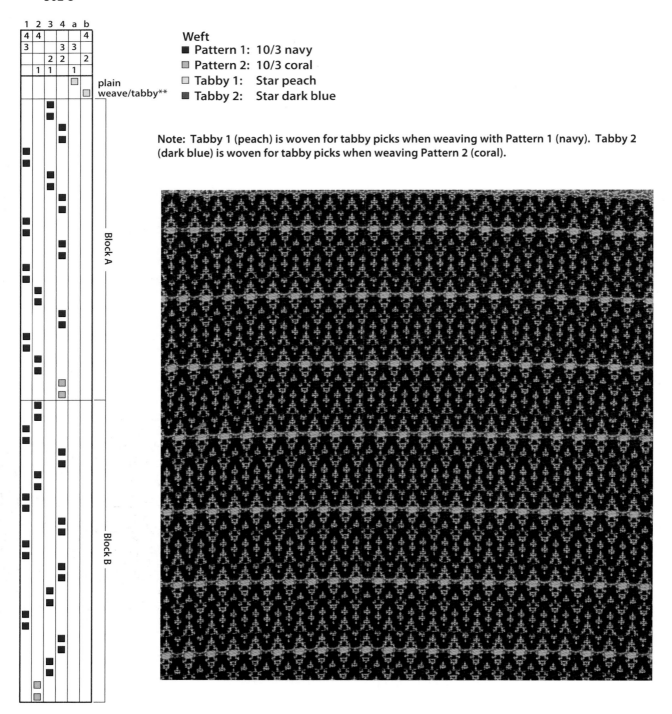

Weft
- ■ Pattern 1: 10/3 navy
- ▨ Pattern 2: 10/3 coral
- ☐ Tabby 1: Star peach
- ■ Tabby 2: Star dark blue

Note: Tabby 1 (peach) is woven for tabby picks when weaving with Pattern 1 (navy). Tabby 2 (dark blue) is woven for tabby picks when weaving Pattern 2 (coral).

302-4

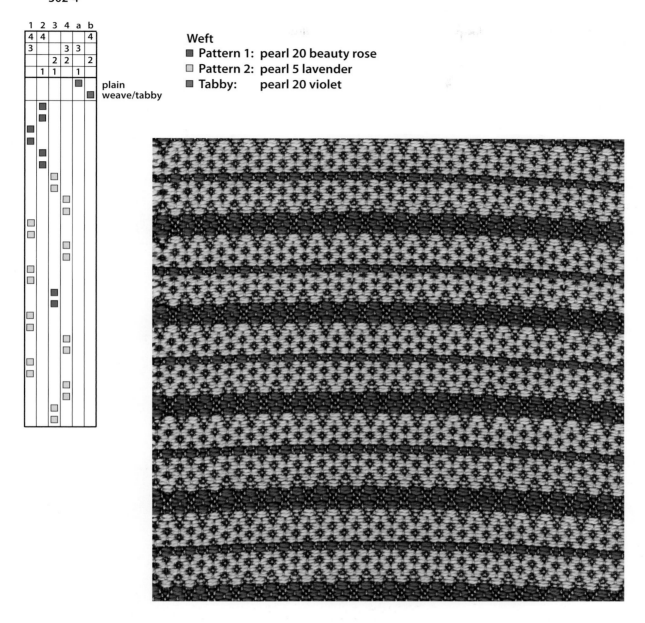

Weft
- ■ Pattern 1: pearl 20 beauty rose
- ☐ Pattern 2: pearl 5 lavender
- ■ Tabby: pearl 20 violet

plain weave/tabby

302-5

Weft
- ■ Pattern 1: 10/3 dark green
- ■ Pattern 2: 10/3 medium green
- ■ Pattern 3: 10/3 lilly green
- □ Pattern 4: 10/3 lemon tint
- □ Tabby: 50/3 beige

Treadling profile draft

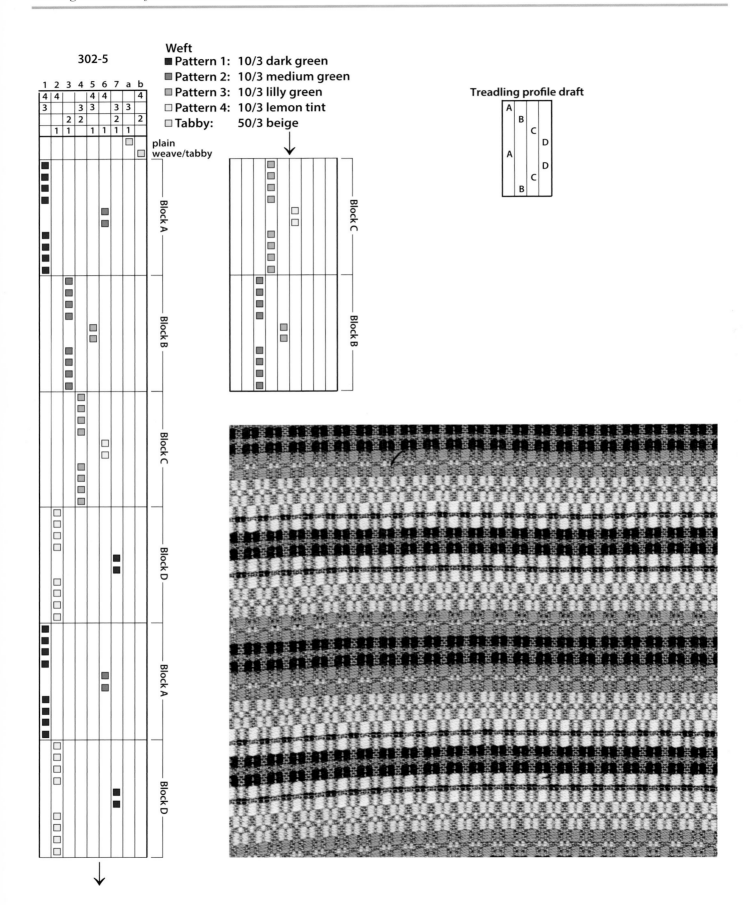

302-6

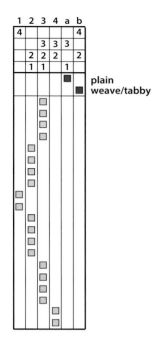

plain
weave/tabby

Weft
☐ **Pattern:** light gray weaving wool
■ **Tabby 1:** dark raspberry
■ **Tabby 2:** Yale blue

Note: There are two tabby wefts used for this sample. The tabby weft
is changed when the pattern treadling sequence is repeated.

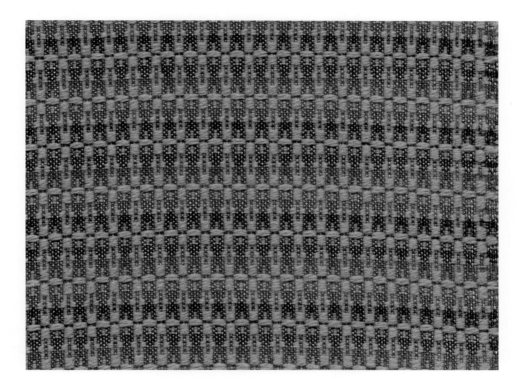

302-7

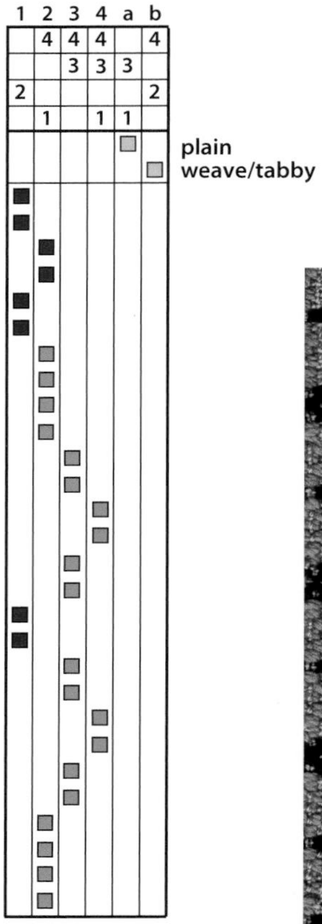

1	2	3	4	a	b
	4	4	4		4
		3	3	3	
2					2
	1		1	1	

plain weave/tabby

Weft

- ■ **Pattern 1:** 10/3 dark brown
- ▪ **Pattern 2:** rose fraise
- ▫ **Tabby:**   Star rose beige

Combination Weaves

Some of Dr. Bateman's samples combined more than one of his weaves into a single sample. The samples included in this section demonstrate different methods he used to combine blocks with different threading sequences. He also explored use of multiple colors within threading blocks.

For more information about Combination weaves, refer to Harvey, Virginia I., *Boulevard, Chevron, and Combination Weaves, Based on Dr. William G. Bateman's Manuscript*, Shuttle Craft Guild Monograph 38 (Freeland, WA: HTH Publishers, 1987).

Warp 110

Weave: Eight-shaft Combination Boulevard-Divided Twill
Sett: 30 epi

Warp: 6-end Boulevard blocks
- 20/2 gray - shaft 1
- 10/3 gray - shaft 2
- lavender floss - shaft 3
- pearl 20 light lavender - shaft 4
- bright rose floss - shaft 5
- pearl 20 light rose - shaft 6
- wine floss - shaft 7
- pearl 20 raspberry - shaft 8

Warp: 14-end Boulevard blocks
- 10/2 gray - shaft 1
- 10/3 gray - shaft 2
- bright rose floss - shaft 3
- pearl 20 purple-navy - shaft 4 through 8

Warp: Divided Twill
- 20/2 gray - shaft 1
- 20/2 navy - shaft 2
- bright rose floss - shaft 3
- lavender floss - shaft 4
- deep lavender floss - shaft 5
- old rose floss - shaft 6
- wine floss - shaft 7
- deep wine floss - shaft 8

Threading blocks

Block D - Boulevard   Block C - Boulevard   Block B - Boulevard   Block A - Boulevard

Block E - Divided Twill

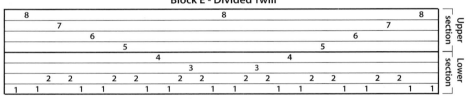

Threading profile draft

Threading repeat

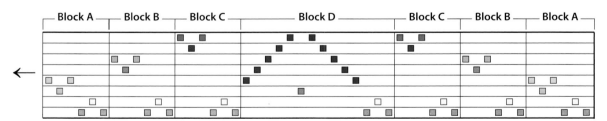

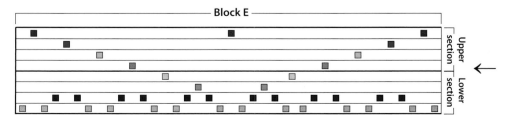

110-1

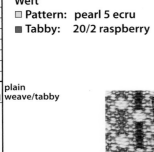

Weft
☐ Pattern: pearl 5 ecru
■ Tabby: 20/2 raspberry

plain
weave/tabby

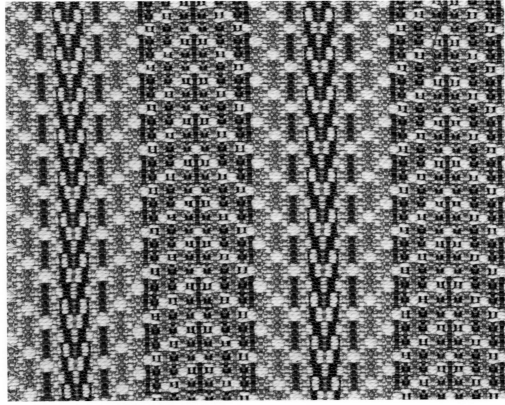

110-2

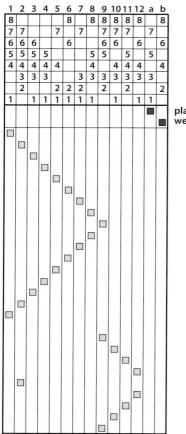

	1	2	3	4	5	6	7	8	9	10	11	12	a	b
8	8					8		8	8	8	8	8		8
7	7	7			7		7		7	7	7		7	
6	6	6	6			6			6	6		6		6
5	5	5	5	5				5	5		5		5	
4	4	4	4	4	4			4		4	4	4		4
3		3	3	3			3	3	3	3	3	3	3	
2					2	2	2		2		2			2
1	1		1	1	1	1	1	1		1		1	1	

plain weave/tabby

Weft

□ **Pattern:** parchment wool

■ **Tabby:** pearl 20 purple-navy

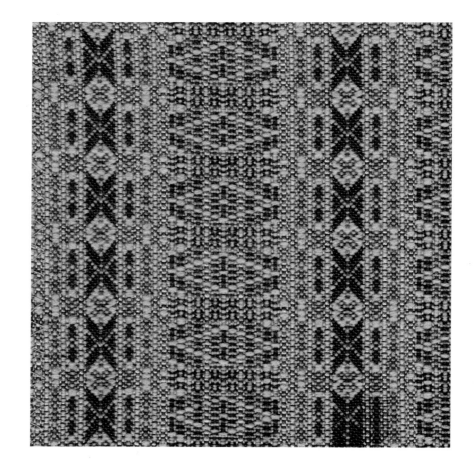

Warp 276

Weave: Eight-shaft Combination Park-Chevron
Sett: 30 epi
Warp: ☐ pearl 10 gold on shaft 3
  ■ pearl 10 light olive on shaft 6 when in center of point sequence
  ☐ 20/2 Egyptian cotton ecru on all other threads

Threading blocks

Block E - Chevron	Block D - Park	Block C - Chevron	Block B - Park	Block A - Chevron

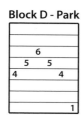
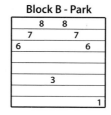
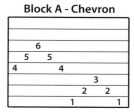

Threading profile draft

Threading repeat

Block E	Block D	Block C	Block B	Block A

276-2

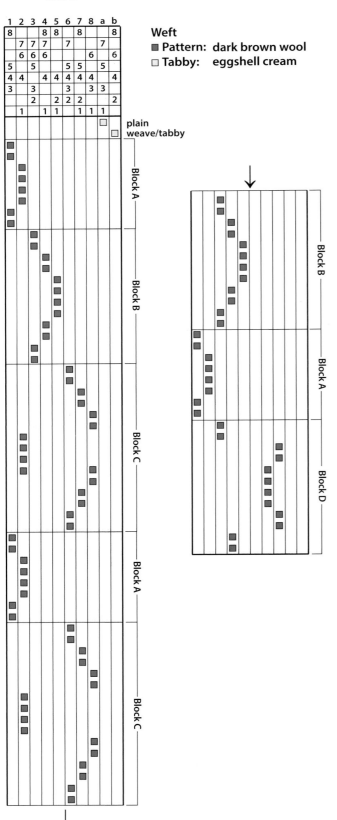

Weft
■ **Pattern:** dark brown wool
□ **Tabby:** eggshell cream

plain weave/tabby

Block A
Block B
Block C
Block A
Block C

Block B
Block A
Block D

Treadling profile draft

276-3

1	2	3	4	5	a	b
			8	8		8
7		7	7		7	
6		6		6		6
	5	5	5	5	5	
	4					4
	3	3		3	3	
2	2		2	2		2
1					1	

Weft

■ **Pattern:**   Reseda green

□ **Tabby:**   pearl 20 light gray

□ plain weave/tabby

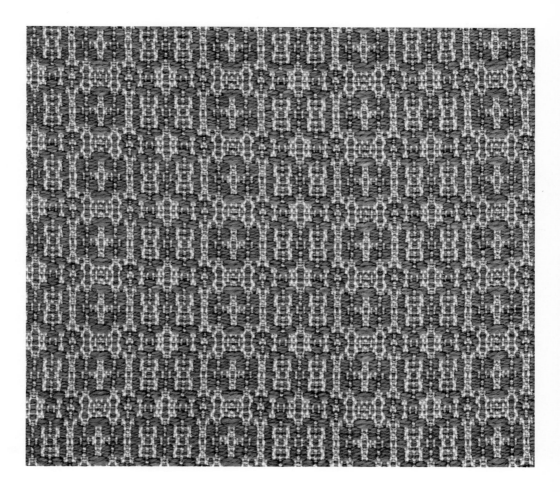

276-4

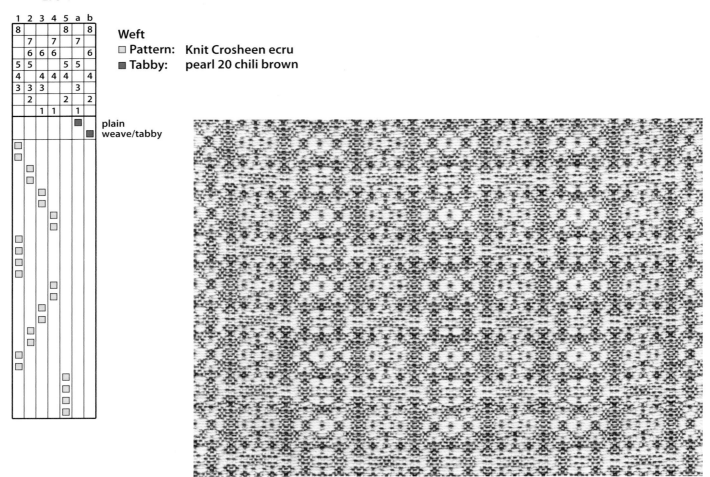

Weft
☐ **Pattern:** Knit Crosheen ecru
■ **Tabby:** pearl 20 chili brown

plain weave/tabby

Warp 385

Weave: Eight-shaft Combination Park-Boulevard-Chevron
Sett: 30 epi
Warp: ☐ 20/2 ecru

Threading blocks

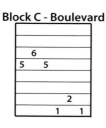

Block D - Park

Block C - Boulevard

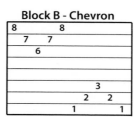

Block B - Chevron

Block A - Chevron

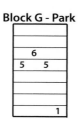

Block H - Boulevard

Block G - Park

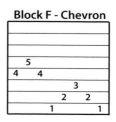

Block F - Chevron

Block E - Chevron

Threading profile draft

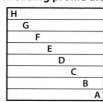

Threading repeat

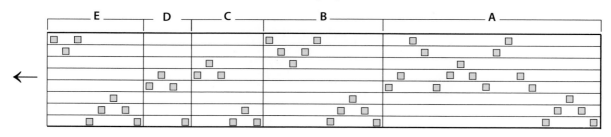

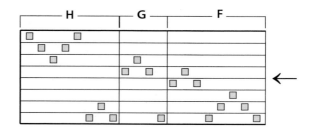

385-1

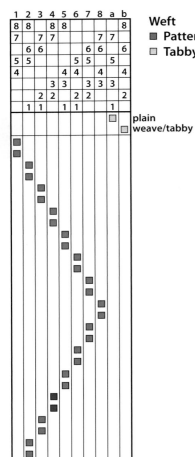

Weft

■ **Pattern:** pearl 5 dark olive

□ **Tabby:** pearl 20 topaz

plain
weave/tabby

385-2

1	2	3	4	5	6	7	8	a	b
8	8		8	8					8
7		7	7				7	7	
	6	6			6	6			6
5	5			5	5			5	
4			4	4		4			4
		3	3			3	3	3	
	2	2			2	2			2
1	1			1	1				1

plain
weave/tabby

Weft
■ **Pattern:** 10/3 red
□ **Tabby:** 24/3 ecru

385-4

Weft
☐ Pattern: 10/3 ecru
▨ Tabby: dark rose pink rayon

☐ plain
▨ weave/tabby

385-6

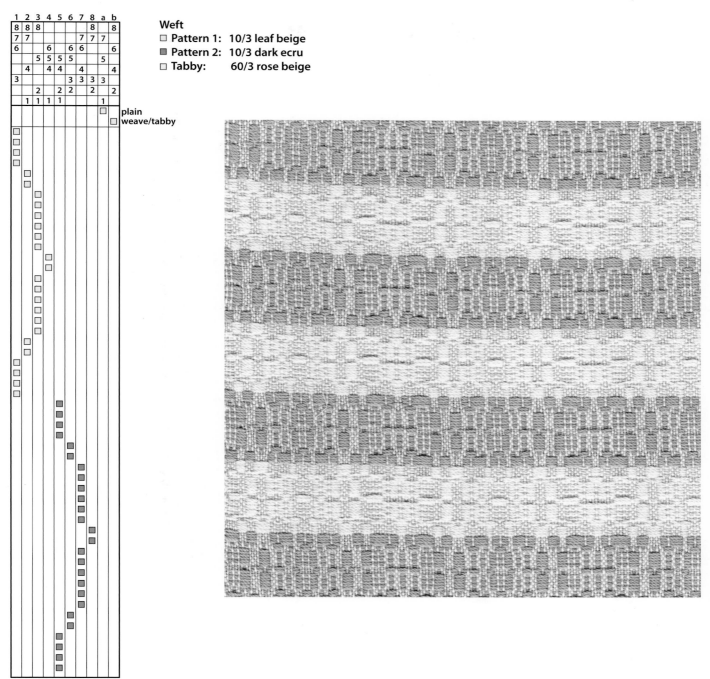

Weft

☐ **Pattern 1:** 10/3 leaf beige

■ **Pattern 2:** 10/3 dark ecru

☐ **Tabby:** 60/3 rose beige

plain weave/tabby

385-7

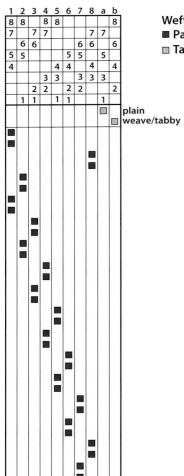

plain weave/tabby

Weft
■ **Pattern:** very dark maroon-brown wool
□ **Tabby:** 60/3 dark beige

Warp 386

Weave: Eight-shaft Combination Park-Chevron

Sett: 30 epi

Warp: Color sequence I

☐ 20/2 dark ecru on 1-2-3-2-1 threading sequence

■ 20/2 gray on five-end straight draw threading sequences and shafts 4 and 5

☐ pearl 10 gold on remaining three ends on shafts 6 and 7 as shown

Warp: Color sequence II

■ 20/2 burnt orange on shafts 6, 7, and 8 straight draw sequences

☐ 20/2 yellow on shafts 1, 3, and 4 and shaft 6 of 6-7-6 sequence

■ pearl 10 light olive on center end of 6-7-8-5-8-7-6 sequence and center end of 6-7-6 sequence

Block E - Park   Block D - Park   Block C - Park   Block B - Chevron   Block A - Chevron

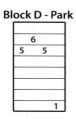

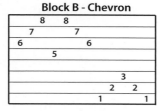
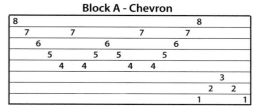

Threading profile draft

E		
	D	
C	C	
		B
		A

Threading blocks

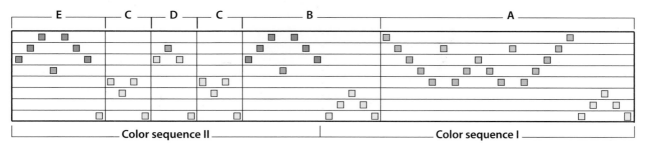

386-1

1	2	3	4	5	6	7	8	a	b
8	8		8	8					8
7		7	7				7	7	
	6	6			6	6		6	
5	5			5	5			5	
4			4	4			4		4
		3	3			3	3	3	
	2	2		2	2				2
	1	1		1	1				1

plain
weave/tabby

Weft
■ **Pattern:** very dark brown wool
☐ **Tabby:** 50/3 cotton beige

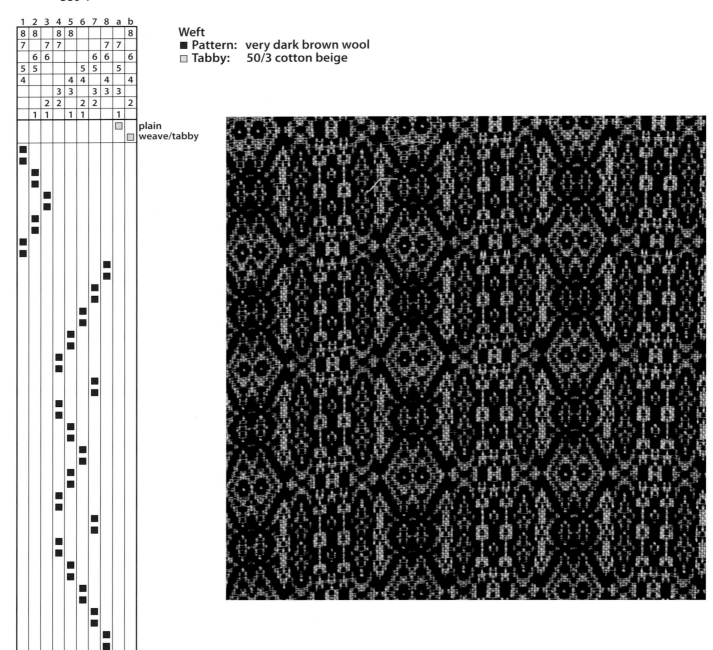

386-3

1	2	3	4	5	6	7	8	a	b
8	8	8			8				8
7	7			7			7	7	
6			6			6	6	6	
		5			5	5	5	5	
	4			4	4	4			4
3			3	3	3			3	3
		2	2	2			2		2
	1	1	1			1			1

□ plain
□ weave/tabby

Weft
■ **Pattern:** pearl 5 dark olive
□ **Tabby:** pearl 20 gold

386-6

	1	2	3	4	5	6	a	b
8	8		8	8		8		8
7	7		7		7		7	
6		6			6			6
5	5			5	5	5		
4	4			4		4		4
3		3	3	3			3	
2	2	2		2	2			2
1	1		1			1		

☐ plain
☐ weave/tabby

Weft
■ **Pattern 1:** 10/3 cotton dark green
■ **Pattern 2:** 10/3 cotton medium green
■ **Pattern 3:** 10/3 cotton burnt orange
☐ **Tabby:** 50/3 cotton dark ecru

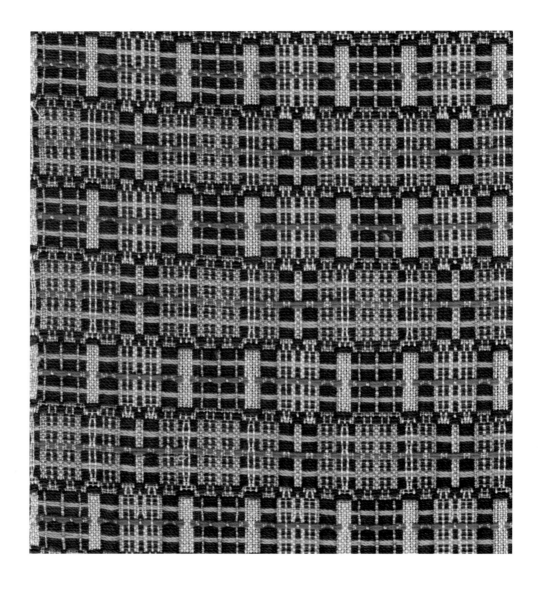

SECTION TWO
TIED WEAVES

Dr. Bateman wove a number of tied weave samples. In this set of samples, all of them are tied weave threadings; however, not all of the samples are woven as a traditional tied weave. For example, instead of using traditional warp ends as ties, Dr. Bateman sometimes used weft picks as ties.

As mentioned earlier in this book, an image of the complete sample is not possible.

In this section, each sample warp shows the following:

- Number assigned by Dr. Bateman
- Tied weave description
- Yarns and colors used for the warp ends
- Sett
- Threading blocks
- Threading profile
- Complete threading repeat

For each sample, the following information is noted:

- Number and sub-number assigned by Dr. Bateman
- Yarns and colors used for weft picks
- Tie-up
- Plain weave and tabby treadles when applicable
- Many of the samples show the treadling sequence with treadling blocks shown by brackets
- A treadling profile if the treadling blocks are not woven in consecutive order

Single Two-tie

Warp 13F

Weave: Seven-shaft Single Two-tie (aka Summer & Winter)
Sett: 30 epi
Warp: ☐ 20/2 mercerized cotton white

Threading block E   Threading block D   Threading block C   Threading block B   Threading block A

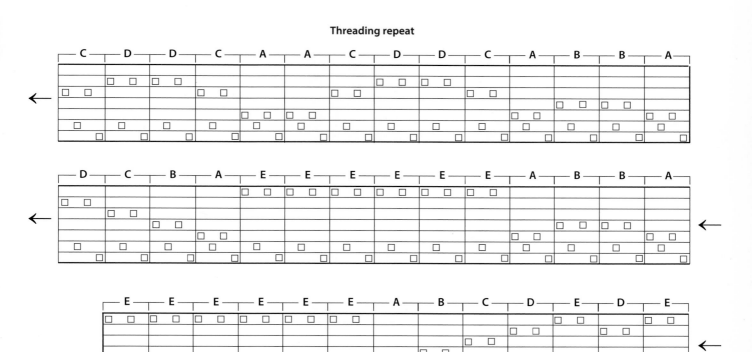

Threading profile draft

Threading repeat

13F-7

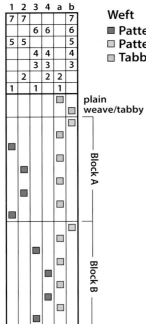

Weft

■ Pattern 1: 10/3 dark green
□ Pattern 2: Beauty-Glo medium blue and silver
□ Tabby: 10/3 cotton gray

Note: Due to the atypical tabby used for this sample (e.g., all tabby picks are done on the same treadle), the weft picks for both the pattern and tabby are shown in the treadling sequence.

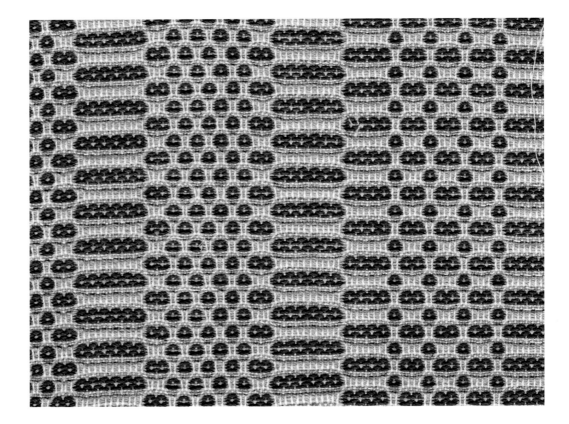

Single Three-tie

Warp 139

Weave: Seven-shaft Single Three-tie
Sett: 30 epi
Warp 1: ☐ 20/2 mercerized cotton sage
Warp 2: ■ pearl 5 Reseda green (shaft four)

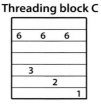

Threading block D / Threading block C / Threading block B / Threading block A

Threading profile draft

Threading repeat

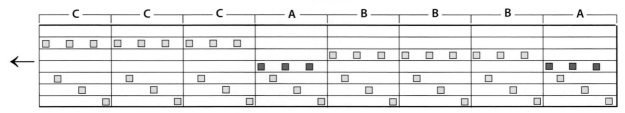

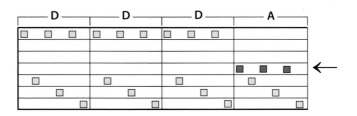

139-1

1	2	3	4	5	6	7	8	9	10	11	12	13	14	15	16	17	18	a	b
						7	7	7	7	7	7	7	7	7	7	7	7		7
6	6	6	6	6	6							6	6	6	6	6	6		6
5	5	5	5	5	5	5	5	5	5	5	5								5
4	4	4				4	4	4				4	4	4					4
	3	3			3	3			3	3			3	3		3	3	3	
2		2	2			2	2			2	2			2	2			2	2
1	1			1	1		1	1			1	1			1	1			1

Weft

- ■ Pattern: pearl 3 cork
- □ Tabby: 20/2 mercerized cotton sage

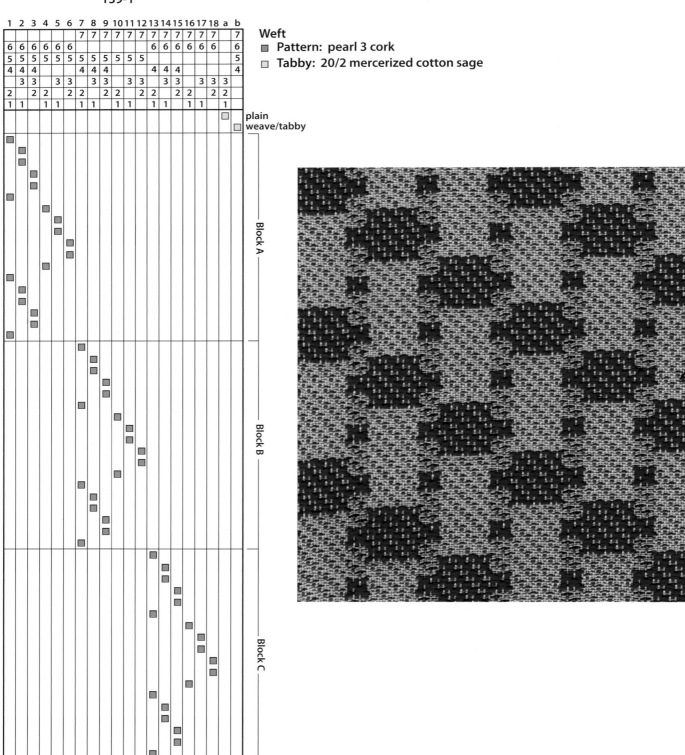

plain
weave/tabby

Block A

Block B

Block C

139-2

Weft
- ☐ Pattern 1: pearl 5 crabapple
- ■ Pattern 2: pearl 5 turquoise
- ■ Pattern 3: pearl 5 light olive
- ☐ Tabby: 20/2 mercerized cotton sage

Note: Due to the atypical tabby used for this sample, the weft picks for both the pattern and tabby are shown in the treadling sequence.

plain weave/tabby

Block A

Block B

Block C

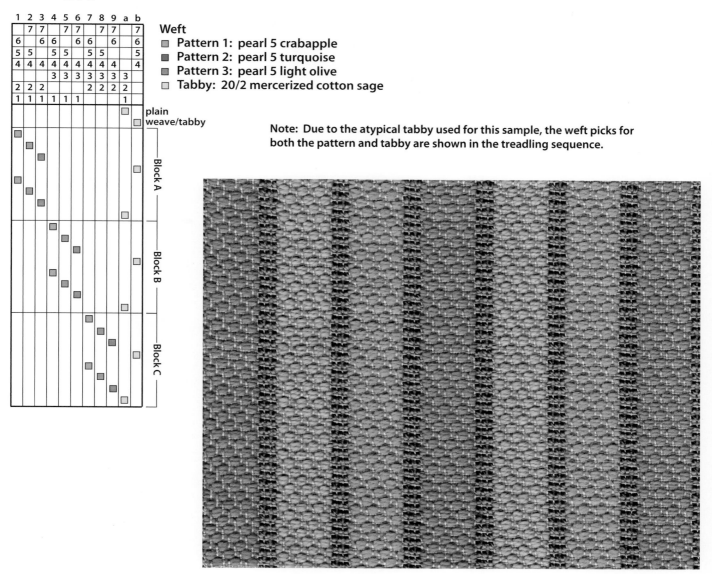

139-3

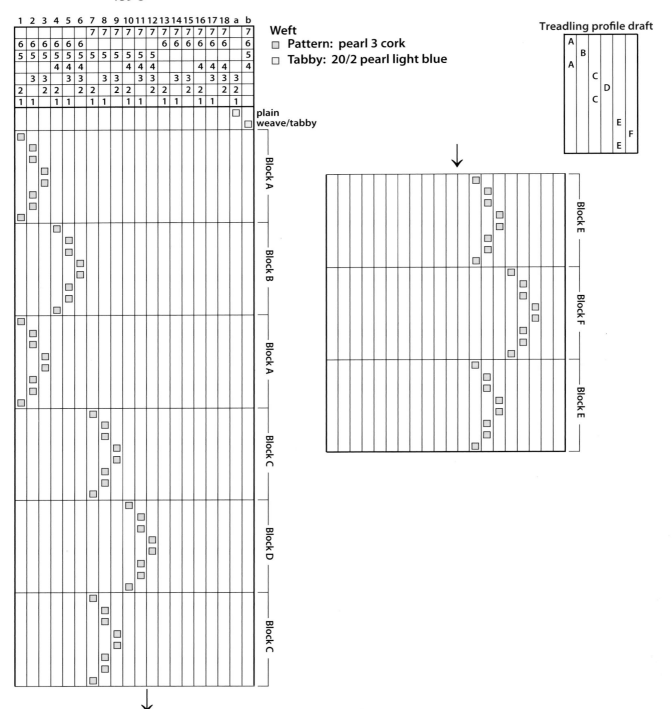

Weaving Innovations from the Bateman Collection

Weft
- ☐ Pattern: pearl 3 cork
- ☐ Tabby: 20/2 pearl light blue

Treadling profile draft

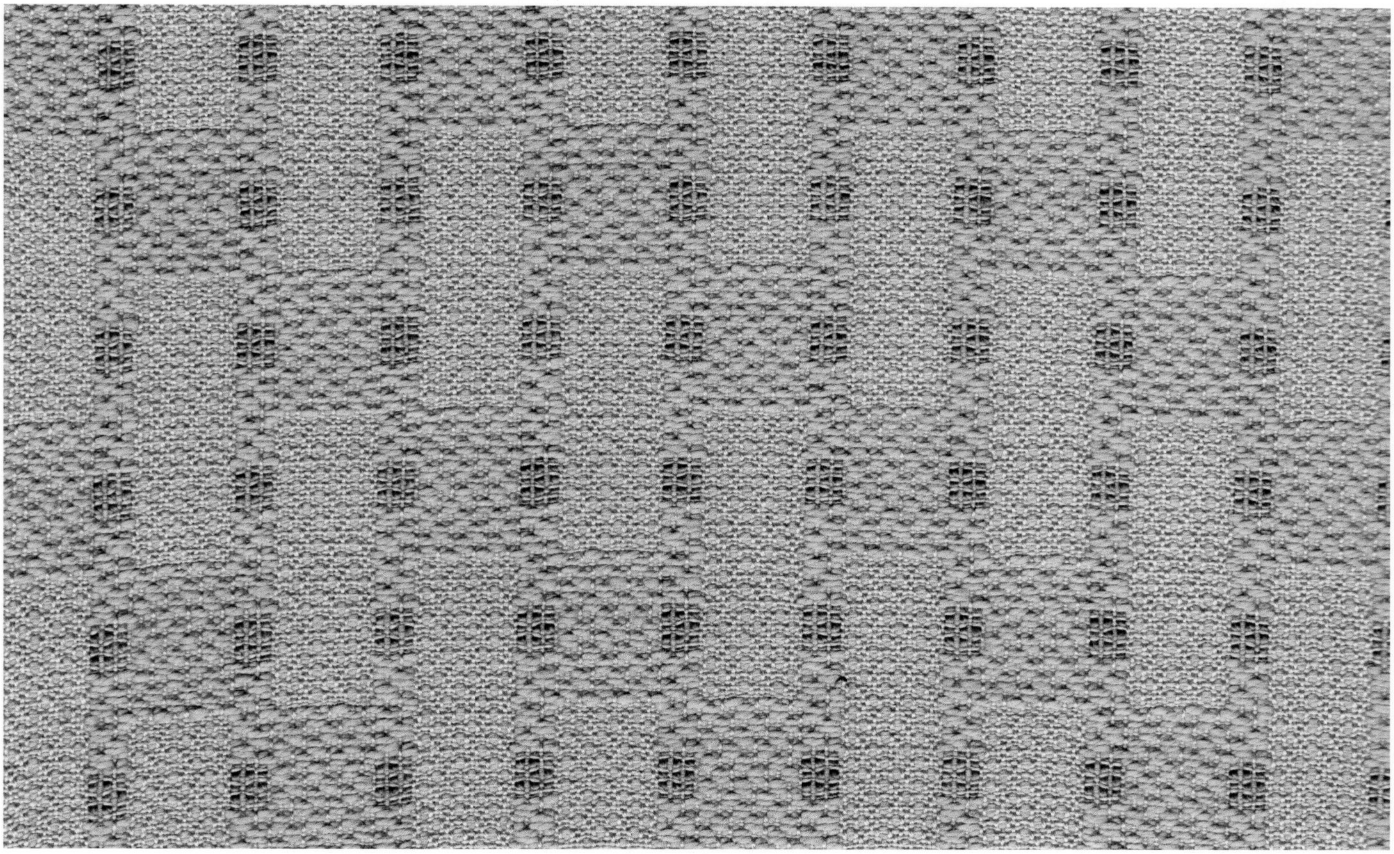

139-4

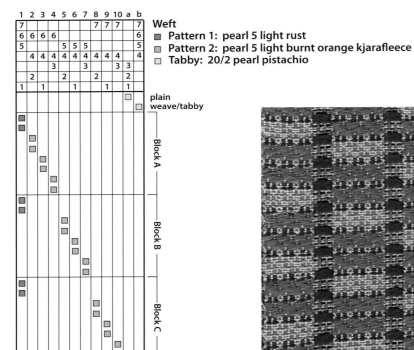

Weft
- ■ Pattern 1: pearl 5 light rust
- ■ Pattern 2: pearl 5 light burnt orange kjarafleece
- □ Tabby: 20/2 pearl pistachio

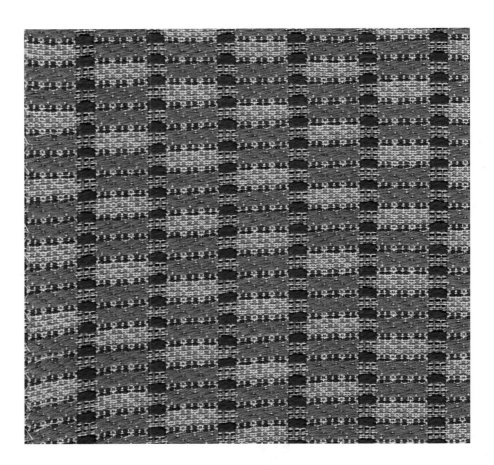

Warp 141

Weave: Seven-shaft Single Three-tie Weave
Sett: 30 epi
Warp: ☐ 20/2 cotton natural

Threading block D

7	7	7	7
	3		
2		2	
			1

Threading block C

6	6	6	6
	3		
2		2	
			1

Threading block B

5	5	5	5
	3		
2		2	
			1

Threading block A

4	4	4	4
	3		
2		2	
			1

Threading profile draft

	D	D			D		D			D	D								
C	C				C	C	C		C	C				C	C				
	B	B								B	B		B	B	B	B		B	B
								A	A		A		A			A	A		

Threading repeat

141-1

Weft

☐ Pattern: old gold weaving wool

☐ Tabby: 20/2 cotton natural

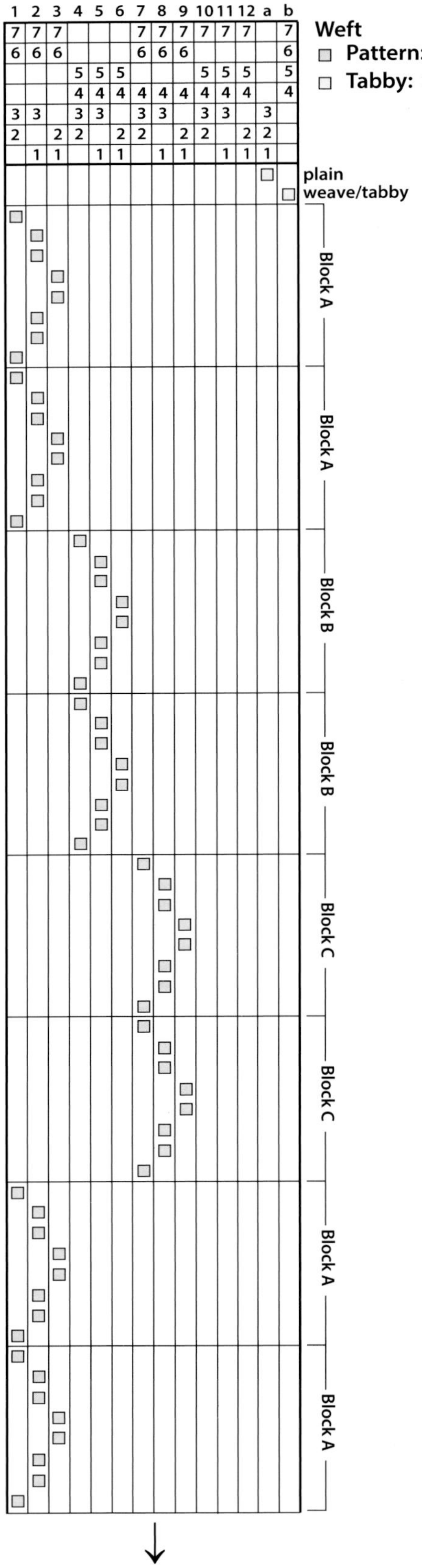

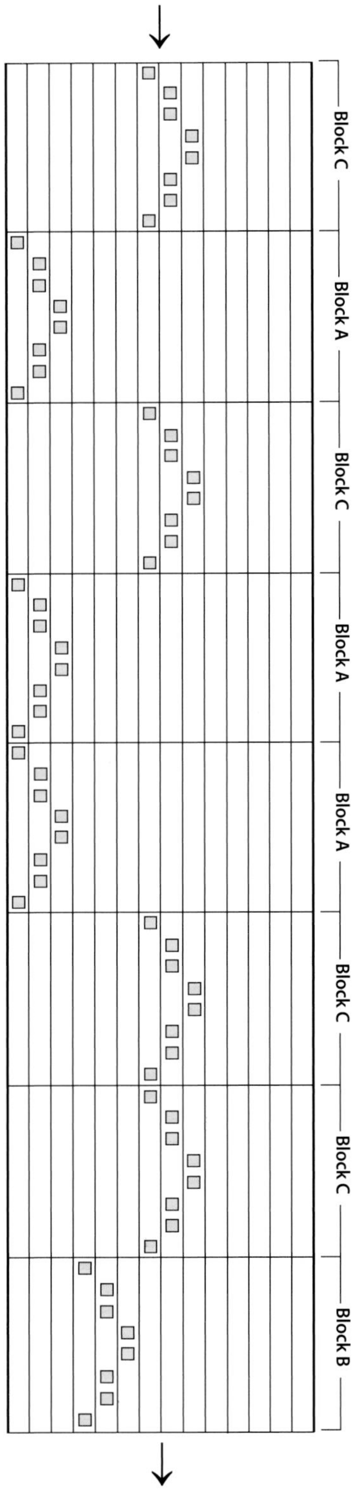

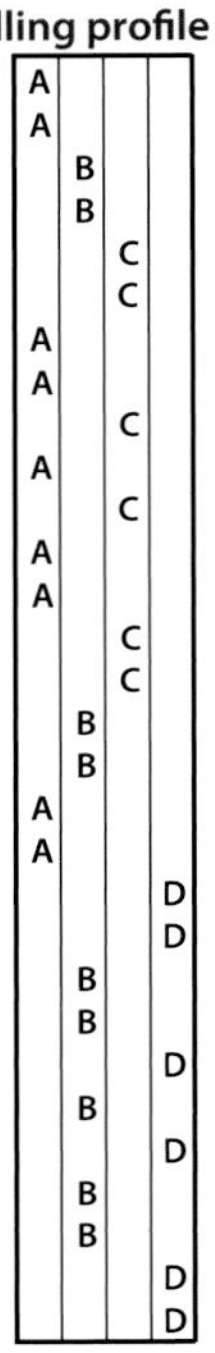

☐ plain
☐ weave/tabby

Treadling profile draft

141-1 (cont)

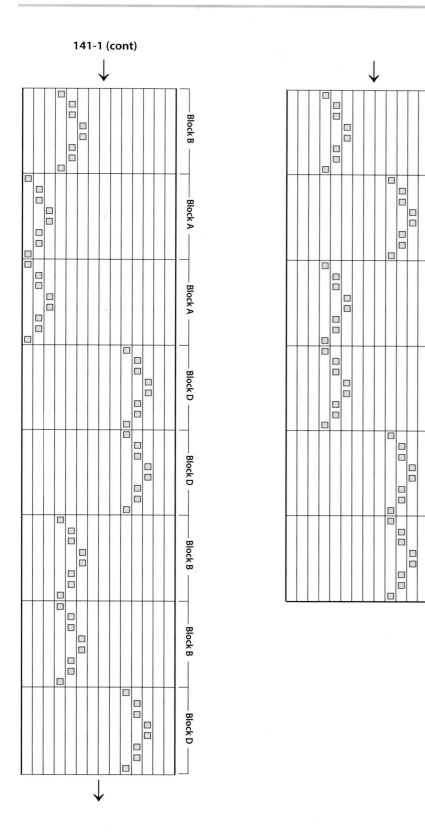

141-2

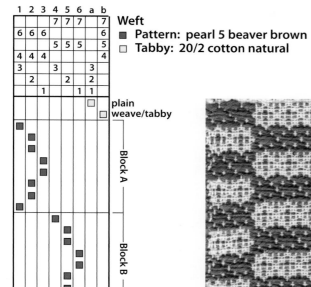

Weft

- ■ Pattern: pearl 5 beaver brown
- □ Tabby: 20/2 cotton natural

plain
weave/tabby

Block A

Block B

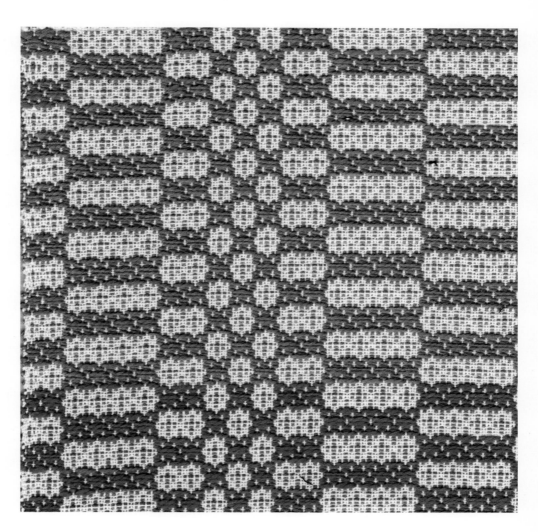

Warp 144

Weave: Eight-shaft Single Three-tie Weave (aka Bergman)
Sett: 30 epi
Warp: ☐ 20/2 cotton natural

Threading block C

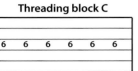

Threading block B

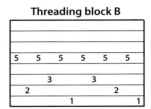

Threading block A

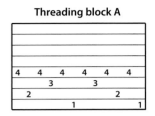

Threading block E

Threading block D

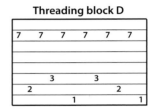

Threading profile draft

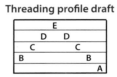

Threading repeat

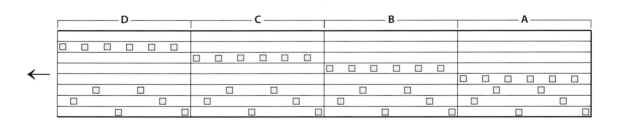

144-5

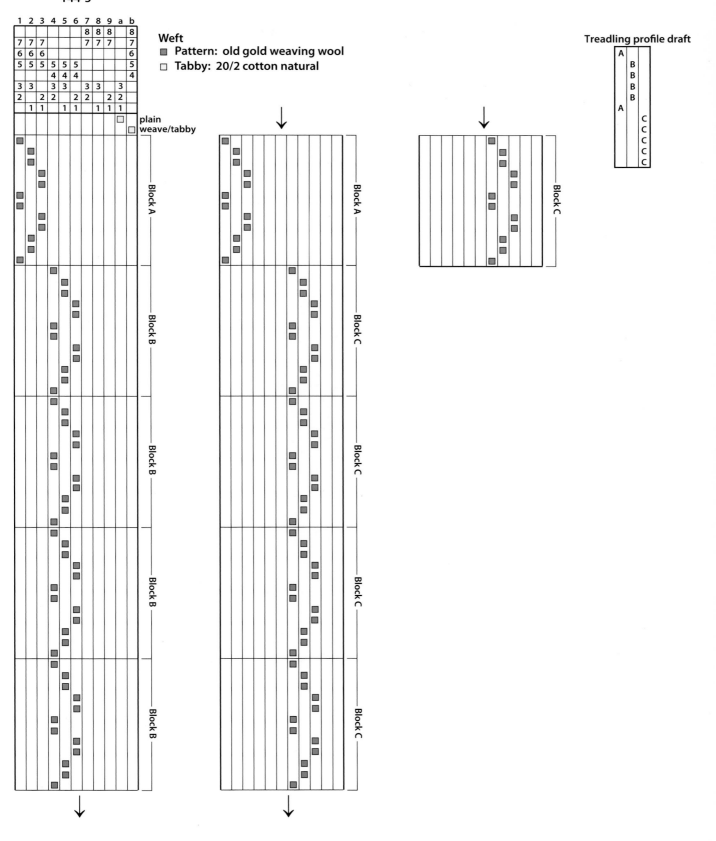

Weft
- ■ Pattern: old gold weaving wool
- □ Tabby: 20/2 cotton natural

plain weave/tabby

Treadling profile draft

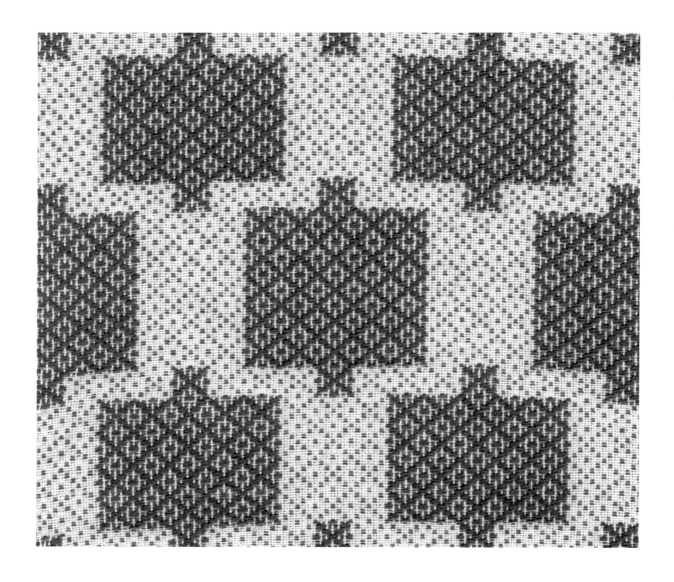

Weft
- ■ Pattern 1: 2 ply worsted black
- ■ Pattern 2: Fabri emerald

144-7 (part 1)

1	2	3	4	5	6	7	8	9	10	11	12	13	14	15	16	17	18	19	20	21	22	23	24	25	26	27	28	29
8		8		8		8		8		8		8		8		8		8		8		8		8		8		8
7		7		7		7			7		7		7		7		7		7		7		7		7		7	
	6		6		6		6	6		6		6		6			6		6		6		6		6		6	
	5		5		5		5	5		5		5		5		5		5		5		5			5		5	
	4		4		4		4	4		4		4		4		4		4		4		4		4		4		4
3	3					3	3	3	3					3	3	3	3					3	3	3	3			
2	2	2	2					2	2	2	2					2	2	2	2					2	2	2	2	
				1	1							1	1							1	1							1

30	31	32	33	34	35	36	37	38	39	40	41	42	43	44	45	46	47	48	49	50	51	52	53	54	55	56	a	b
	8			8		8		8		8		8		8		8		8	8		8		8		8			8
7		7		7		7		7		7	7		7		7		7		7		7		7		7			7
6		6	6		6		6		6		6		6		6		6			6		6		6		6		6
5		5	5		5		5		5		5		5		5		5			5		5		5		5		5
	4		4		4		4		4			4		4		4		4	4		4		4		4			4
	3	3	3	3					3	3	3	3					3	3	3	3					3	3	3	
			2	2	2	2					2	2	2	2					2	2	2	2					2	
1							1	1							1	1							1	1			1	

plain weave
Block A
Block B
Block C
Block D

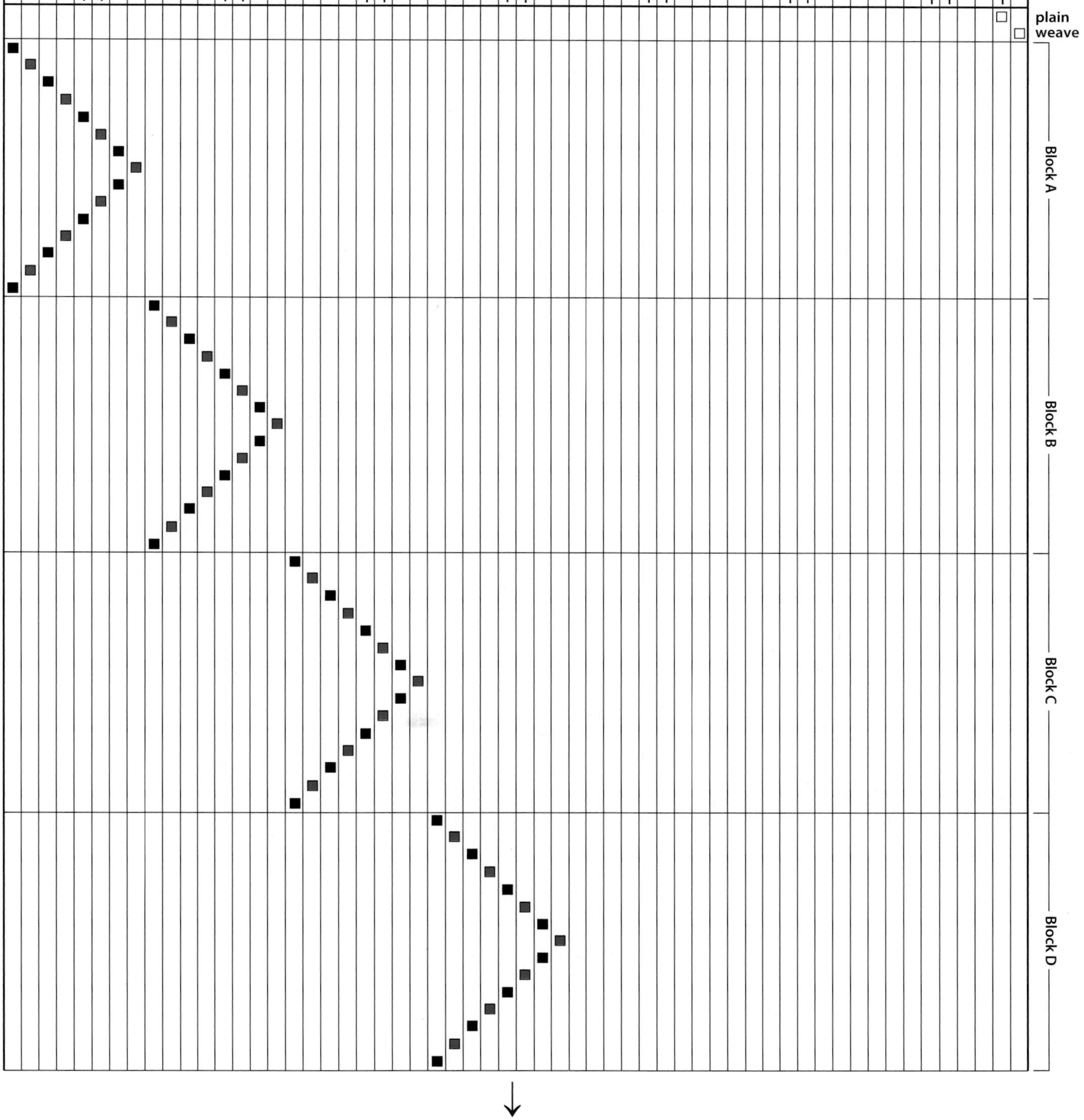

144-7 (part 2)

144-7 (part 3)

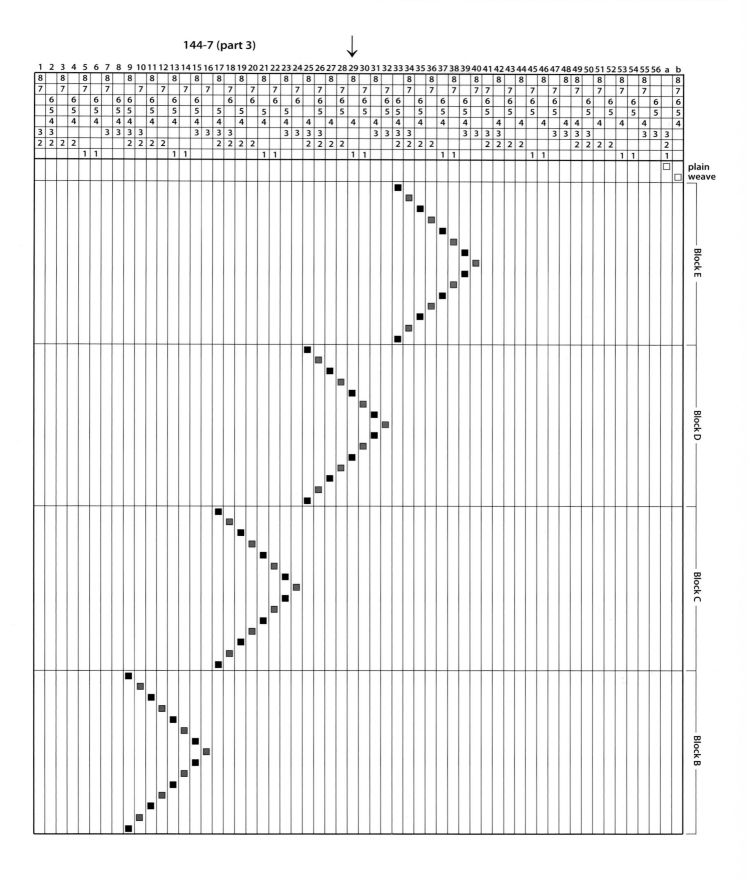

Treadling profile draft

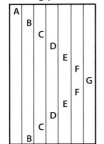

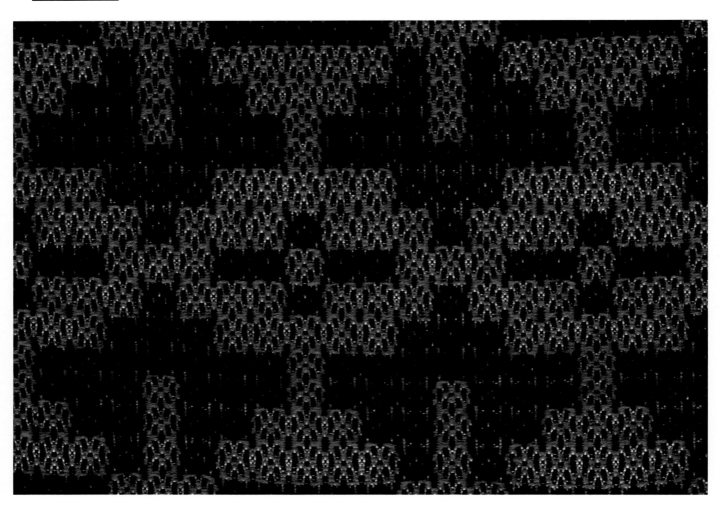

144-8

	1	2	a	b
	8	8		8
	7	7		7
	6	6		6
	5	5		5
	4	4		
	3		3	
		2	2	
	1		1	

Weft
- ☐ Pattern 1: 10/3 cotton ming gold
- ☐ Pattern 2: 10/3 cotton rose fraise
- ☐ Tabby: 20/2 cotton natural

plain weave/tabby

Block A
Block B
Block C
Block B
Block A
Block D
Block A

Block B
Block C
Block B

Treadling profile draft

A
B
B
A
A
B
B
C
C
D

Note: Due to the atypical tabby used for this sample (e.g., all tabby picks are done on the same treadle), the weft picks for both the pattern and tabby are shown in the treadling sequence.

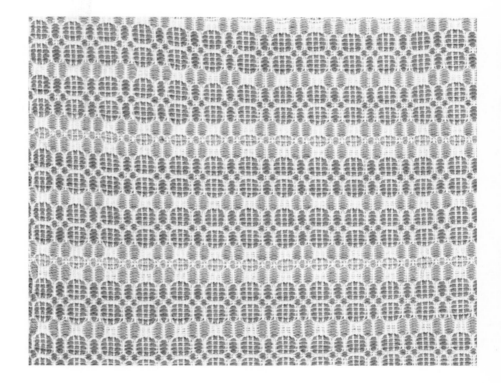

Warp 146

Weave: Seven-shaft Single Three-tie
Sett: 30 epi
Warp: ☐ 20/2 Umbrian (Bernat) buff

Threading block B

5	5	5	5	5	5	5	5
3		3		3			
2		2					
	1		1			1	

Threading block A

4	4	4	4	4	4	4	4
3		3		3			
2		2					
	1		1			1	

Threading block D

7	7	7	7	7	7	7	7
3		3		3			
2		2					
	1		1			1	

Threading block C

6	6	6	6	6	6	6	6
3		3	3				
2		2		2			
	1		1		1		

Threading profile draft

D
C
B
A

Threading repeat

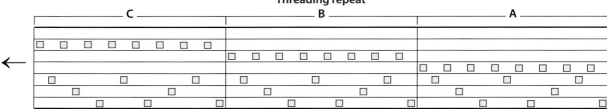

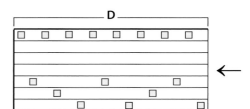

146-2

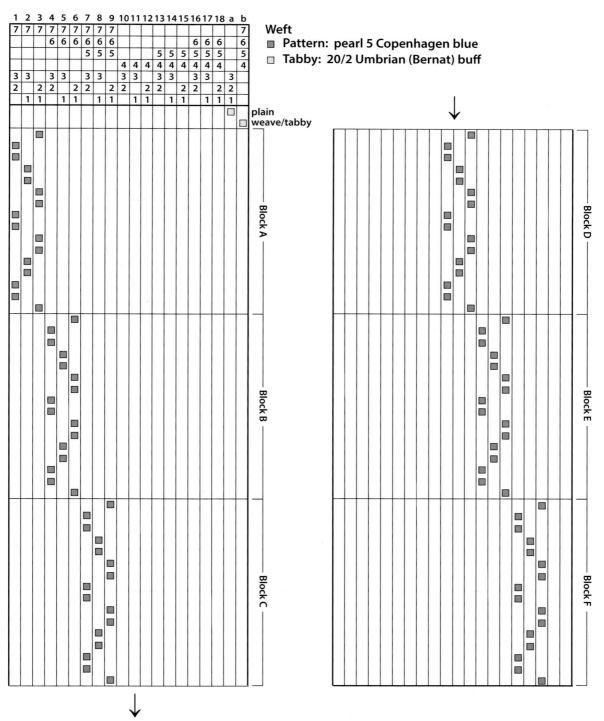

	1	2	3	4	5	6	7	8	9	10	11	12	13	14	15	16	17	18	a	b
	7	7	7	7	7	7	7	7	7											7
			6	6	6	6	6	6								6	6	6		6
					5	5	5						5	5	5	5	5	5		5
							4	4	4	4	4	4	4	4	4	4	4	4		4
	3	3			3	3		3	3			3	3		3	3	3			3
	2		2	2		2	2		2	2		2	2		2	2		2	2	
		1	1		1	1		1	1		1	1		1	1		1	1	1	

Weft

■ Pattern: pearl 5 Copenhagen blue

□ Tabby: 20/2 Umbrian (Bernat) buff

plain
weave/tabby

Block A

Block B

Block C

Block D

Block E

Block F

146-3

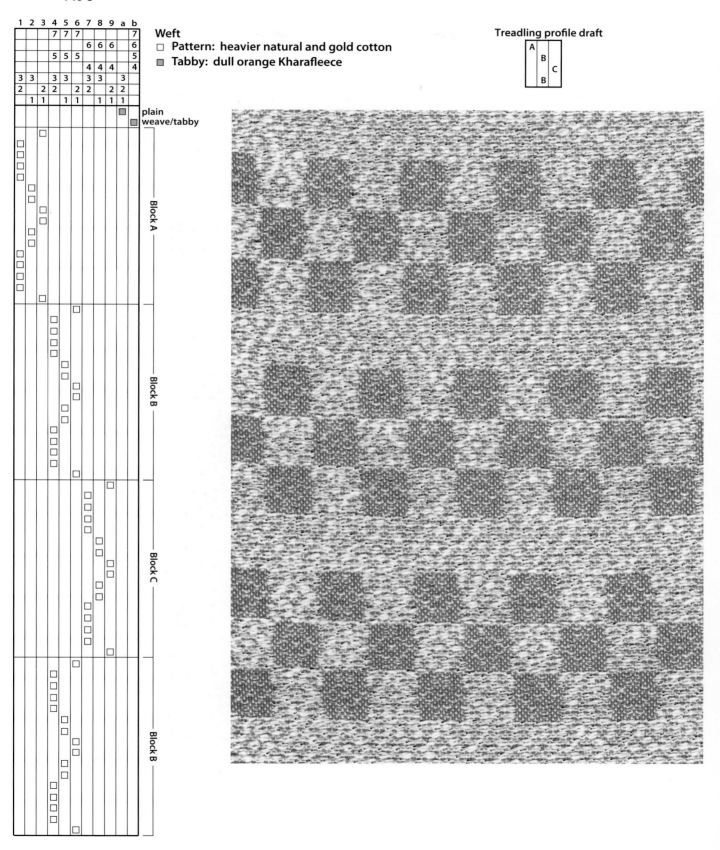

Weft
- ☐ Pattern: heavier natural and gold cotton
- ◼ Tabby: dull orange Kharafleece

Treadling profile draft

A		
	B	
		C
	B	

146-4 (part 1)

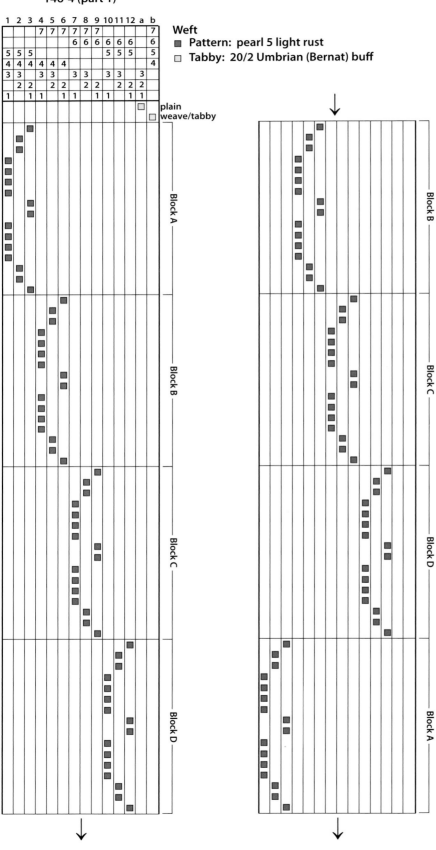

Weft
- ■ Pattern: pearl 5 light rust
- □ Tabby: 20/2 Umbrian (Bernat) buff

□ plain
□ weave/tabby

Treadling profile draft

146-4 (part 2)

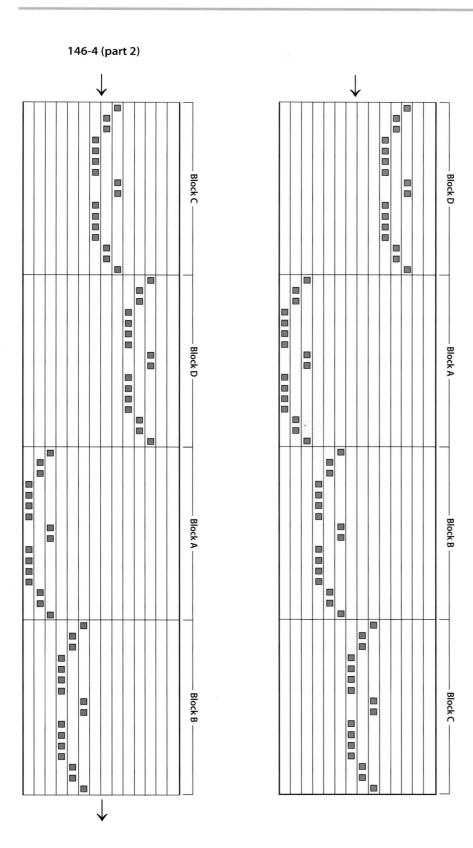

146-8

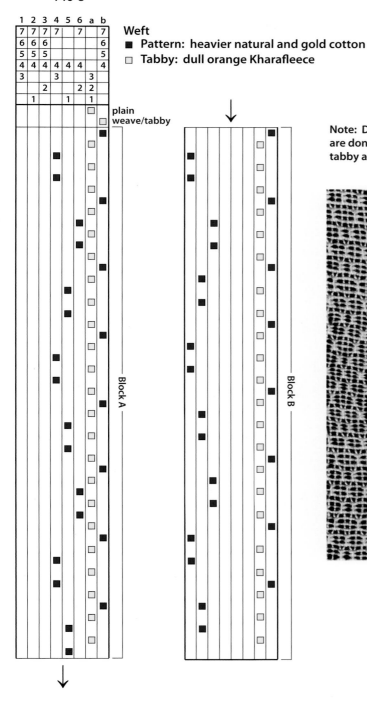

Weft

■ Pattern: heavier natural and gold cotton

□ Tabby: dull orange Kharafleece

Block A

Block B

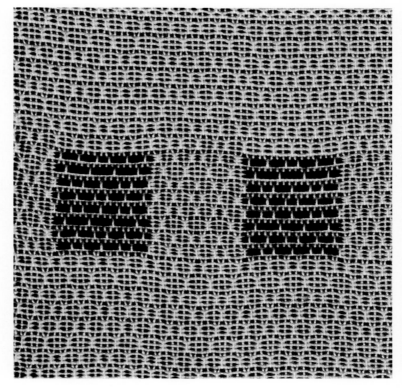

Note: Due to the atypical tabby used for this sample (e.g., all tabby picks are done on the same treadle), the weft picks for both the pattern and tabby are shown in the treadling sequence.

Single Four-tie

Warp 52

Weave: Six-shaft Single Four-tie
Sett: 30 epi
Warp: ☐ **pearl 20 ecru**

Threading block B

6		6		6		6		6		6		6		6		6		6		6		6		6	
										4				4											
				3		3		3								3		3		3					
2		2																		2		2			
									1															1	

Threading block A

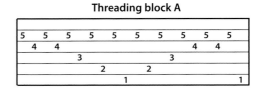

Threading profile draft

B
A

Threading repeat

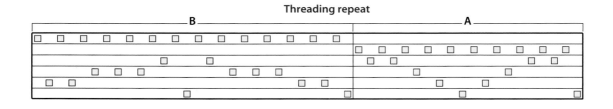

52-1

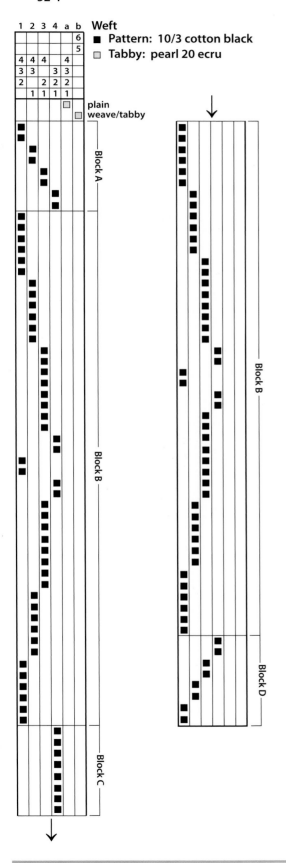

Weft
- ■ Pattern: 10/3 cotton black
- □ Tabby: pearl 20 ecru

Treadling profile draft

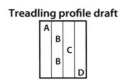

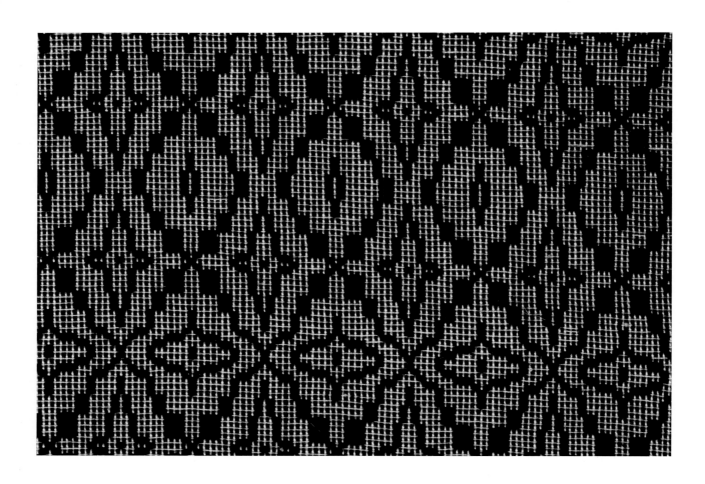

52-2

Weft
- ■ Pattern: pearl 5 skipper blue
- □ Tabby: pearl 20 ecru

Treadling profile draft

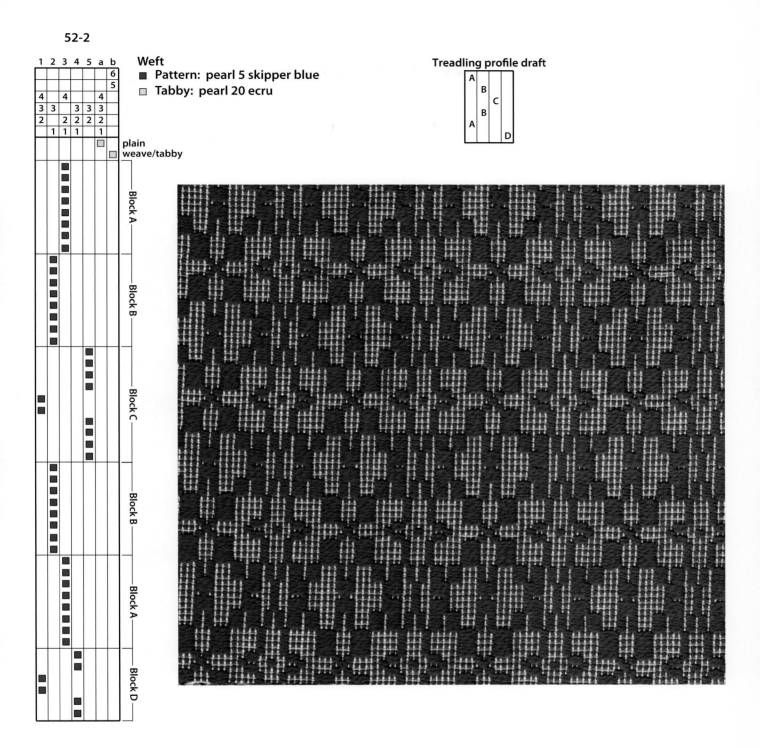

52-7

1	2	3	4	5	a	b	
						6	
						5	
4		4			4		
3	3		3	3	3		
2		2	2	2	2		
	1	1	1		1		

Weft

- ▦ Pattern 1: 10/3 rose fraise (doubled)
- ■ Pattern 2: American Beauty Bucilla (doubled)
- ☐ Tabby: pearl 20 ecru

Treadling profile draft

plain weave/tabby

Block A
Block B
Block C
Block B
Block A
Block D

Note: Due to the atypical tabby used for this sample (e.g., all tabby picks are done on the same treadle), the weft picks for both the pattern and tabby are shown in the treadling sequence.

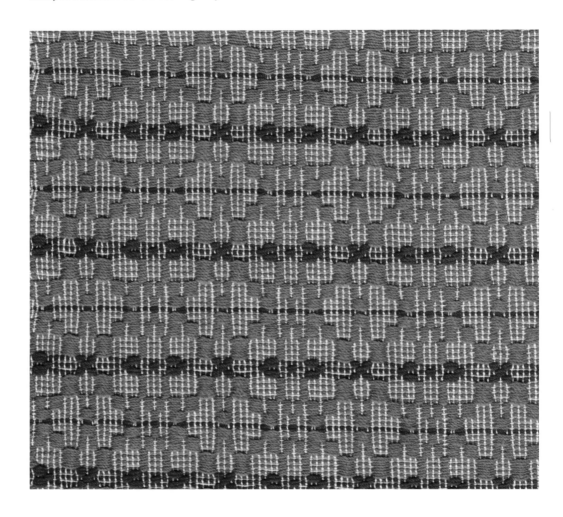

52-12

Weft
- ■ Pattern: 10/3 black
- ☐ Tabby: 10/3 gold

Treadling profile draft

Note: Due to the atypical tabby used for this sample (e.g., all tabby picks are done on the same treadle), the weft picks for both the pattern and tabby are shown in the treadling sequence.

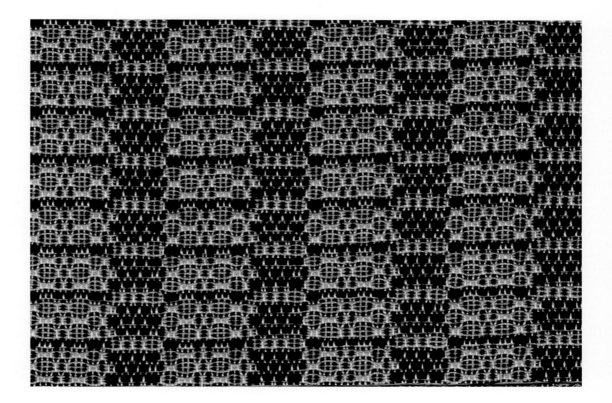

52-13

Weft
- ■ Pattern: 10/3 dark green
- □ Tabby: 10/3 yellow

□ plain weave/tabby

Note: Due to the atypical tabby used for this sample (e.g., all tabby picks are done on the same treadle), the weft picks for both the pattern and tabby are shown in the treadling sequence.

Treadling profile draft

Block A

Block B

Block C

Block B

Block D

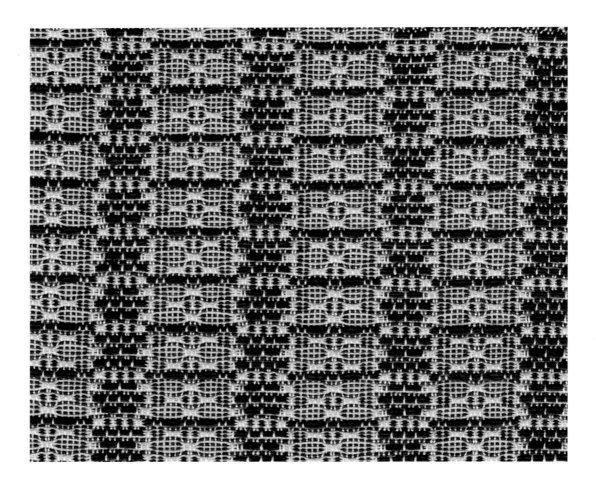

Warp 53

Weave: Eight-shaft Single Four-tie Weave
Sett: 30 epi
Warp: □ pearl 20 ecru

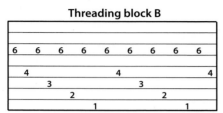

Threading block B

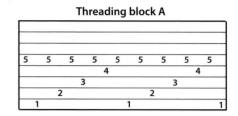

Threading block A

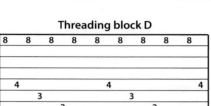

Threading block D

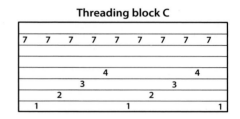

Threading block C

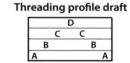

Threading profile draft

Threading repeat

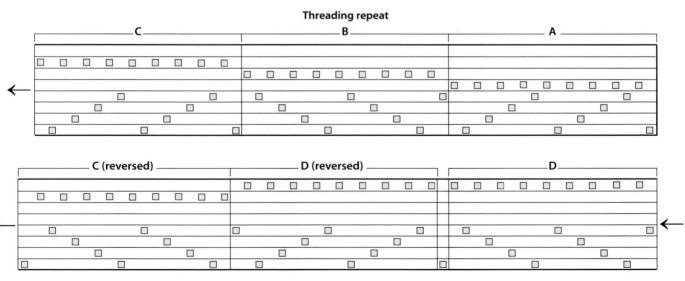

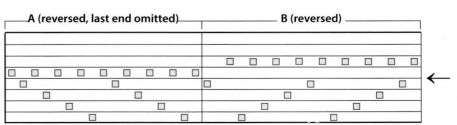

53-1

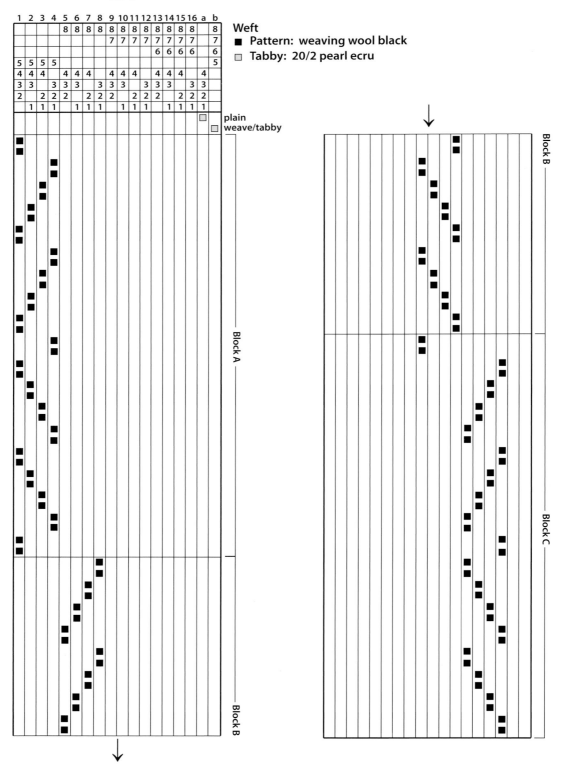

Weft
- ■ Pattern: weaving wool black
- □ Tabby: 20/2 pearl ecru

53-2

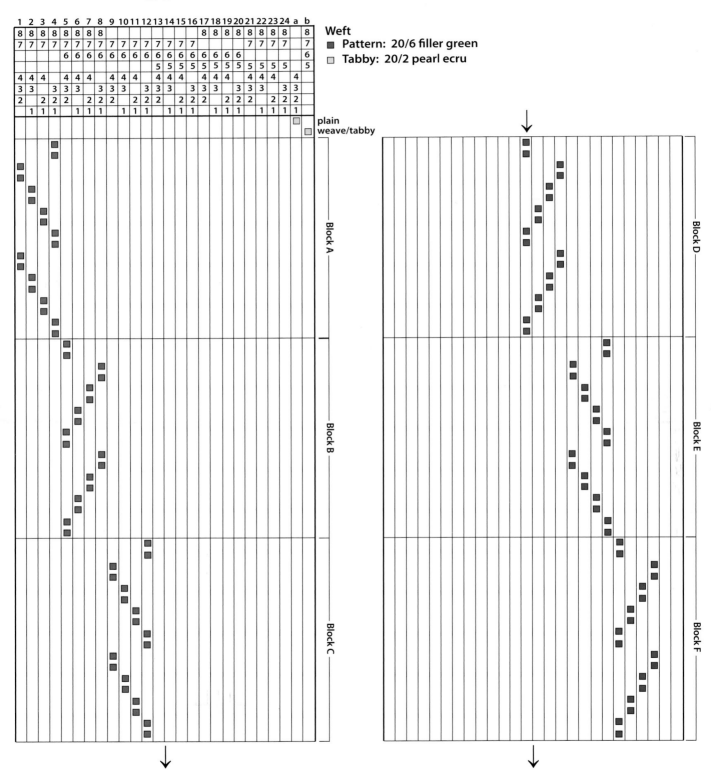

Weft
- ■ Pattern: 20/6 filler green
- ☐ Tabby: 20/2 pearl ecru

☐ plain
☐ weave/tabby

Block A
Block B
Block C
Block D
Block E
Block F

53-2 (continued)

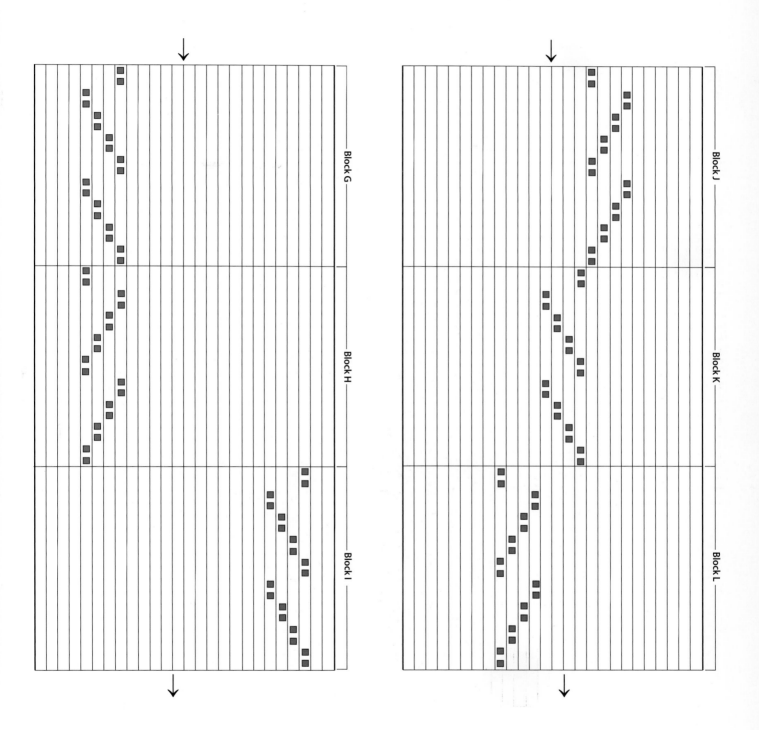

53-2 (continued)

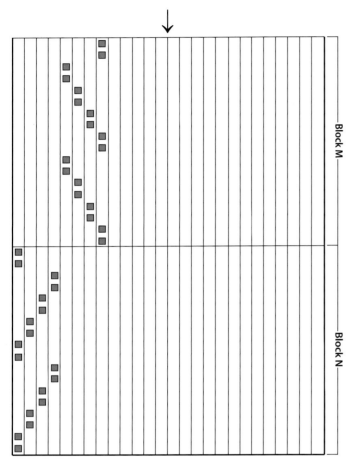

Block M

Block N

53-3

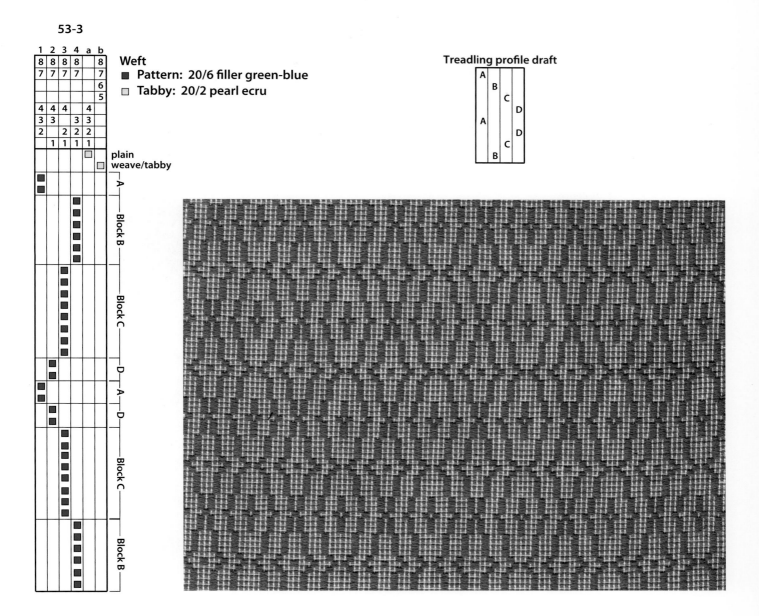

Weft
- ■ Pattern: 20/6 filler green-blue
- □ Tabby: 20/2 pearl ecru

Treadling profile draft

53-7

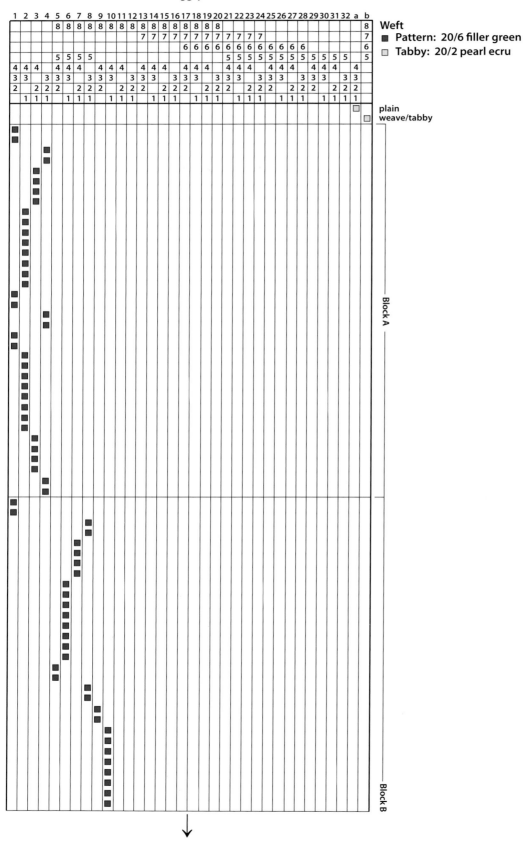

Weft
■ Pattern: 20/6 filler green
□ Tabby: 20/2 pearl ecru

plain weave/tabby

Block A

Block B

53-7 (continued)

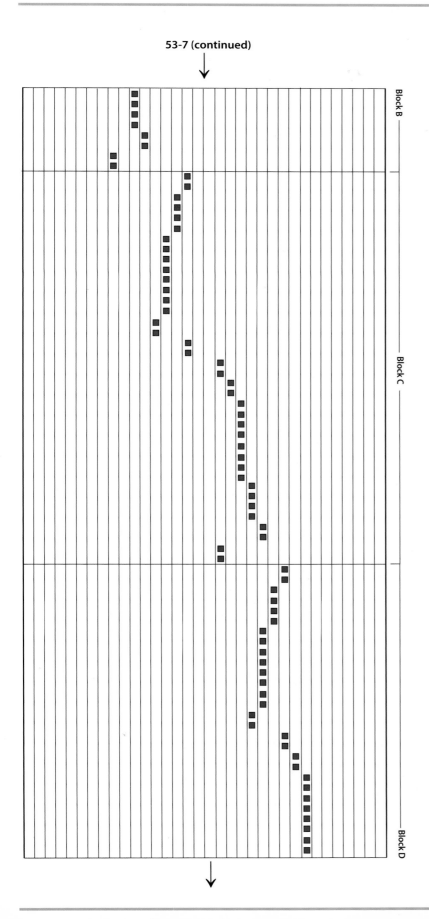

53-7 (continued)

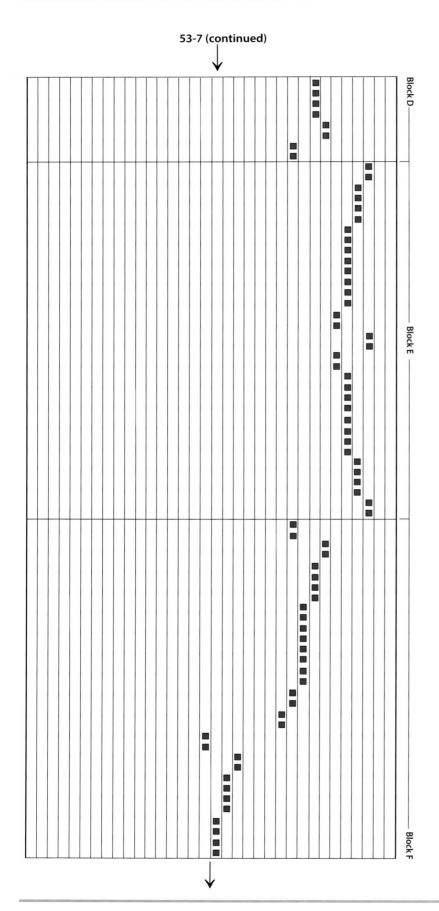

53-7 (continued)

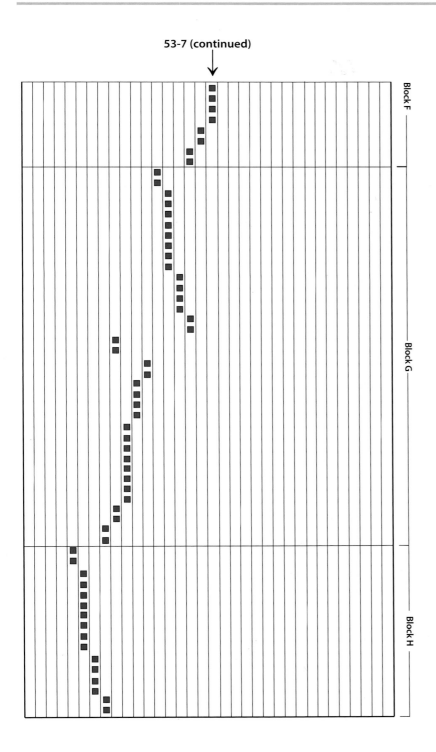

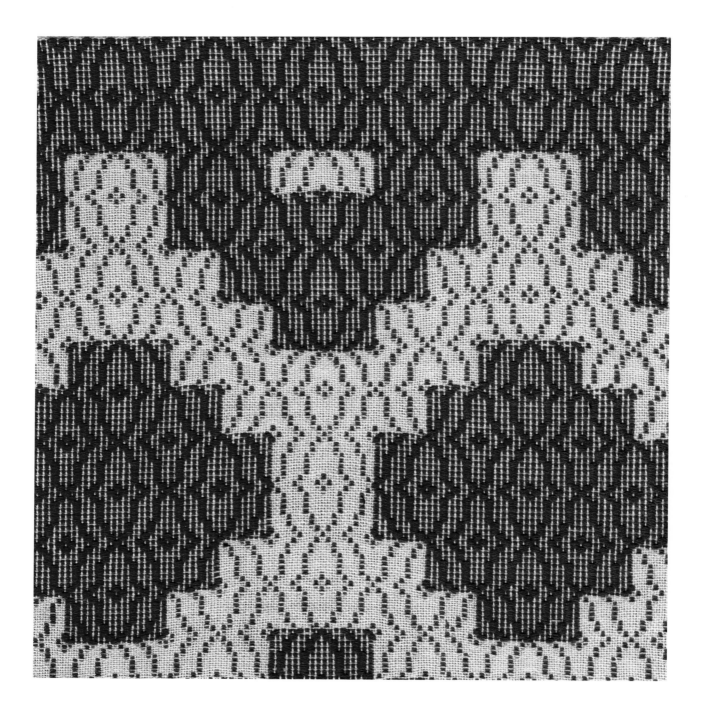

Warp 152

Weave: Eight-shaft Single Four-tie Weave
Sett: 30 epi
Warp: □ 20/2 Egyptian cotton natural

Threading block D

8	8	8	8
4			
	3		
		2	
			1

Threading block C

7	7	7	7
4			
	3		
		2	
			1

Threading block B

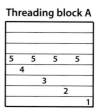

Threading block A

	5	5	5	5
	4			
		3		
			2	
				1

Threading profile draft

D D D		D D D	
	C		
		B	
	A A A		A A A

Threading repeat

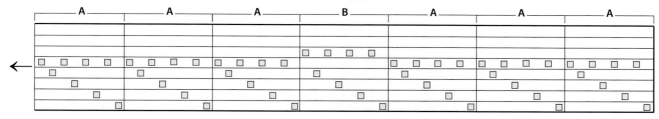

152-1

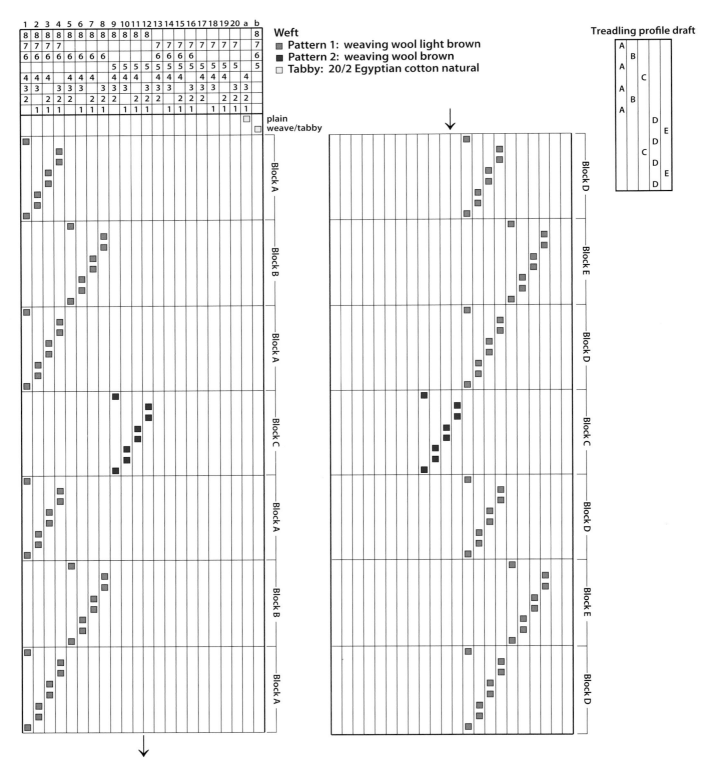

Weft

- ■ Pattern 1: weaving wool light brown
- ■ Pattern 2: weaving wool brown
- □ Tabby: 20/2 Egyptian cotton natural

Treadling profile draft

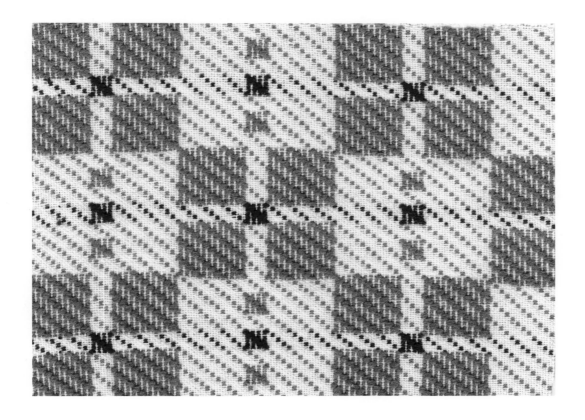

152-2

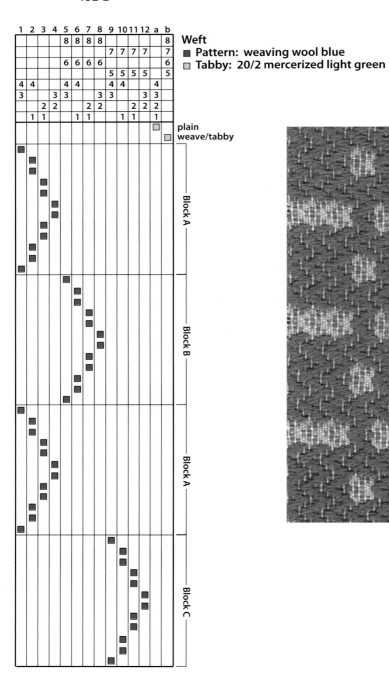

Weft
■ Pattern: weaving wool blue
□ Tabby: 20/2 mercerized light green

Treadling profile draft

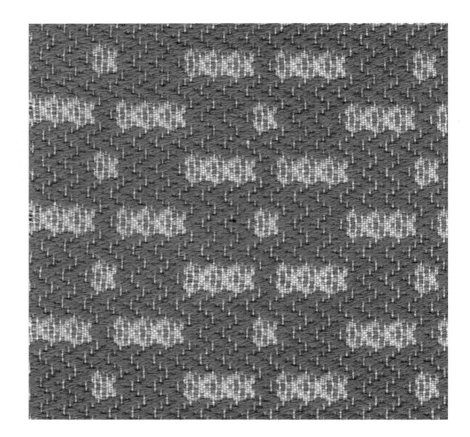

152-3

1	2	3	4	a	b
8	8	8	8		8
7		7			7
6		6			6
		5		5	5
			4		
3	3	3			3
			2		
1	1		1	1	

Weft
- ■ **Pattern 1:** blue stranded filler
- □ **Pattern 2:** pearl 5 dusty rose
- ■ **Pattern 3:** wine cotton novelty
- □ **Tabby:** pearl 20 turquoise

plain
weave/tabby

Note: Due to the atypical tabby used for this sample, the weft picks for both the pattern and tabby are shown in the treadling sequence.

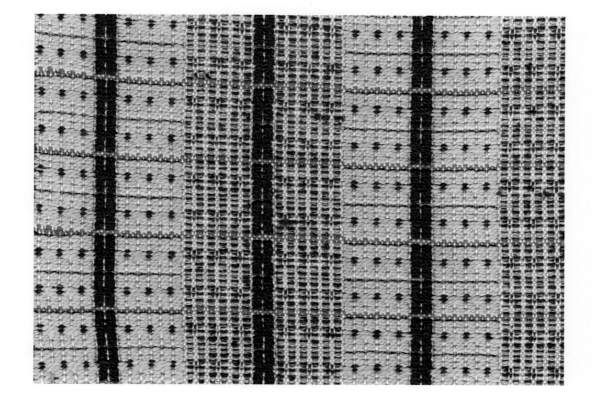

Warp 155

Weave: Eight-shaft Single Four-tie Weave (aka Quigley Diamond)
Sett: 30 epi
Warp: ☐ 20/2 cotton coral

Threading block D

8	8	8	8	8	8
		4			
	3		3		
2				2	
					1

Threading block C

7	7	7	7	7	7
		4			
	3		3		
2				2	
					1

Threading block B

6	6	6	6	6	6
		4			
	3		3		
2				2	
					1

Threading block A

5	5	5	5	5	5
		4			
	3		3		
2				2	

Threading profile draft

	D		D		
	C		C	C	
B				B	B
				A	A

Threading repeat

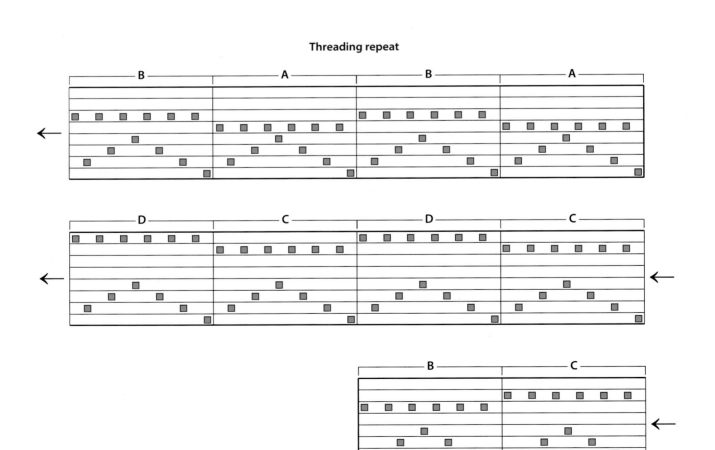

155-2

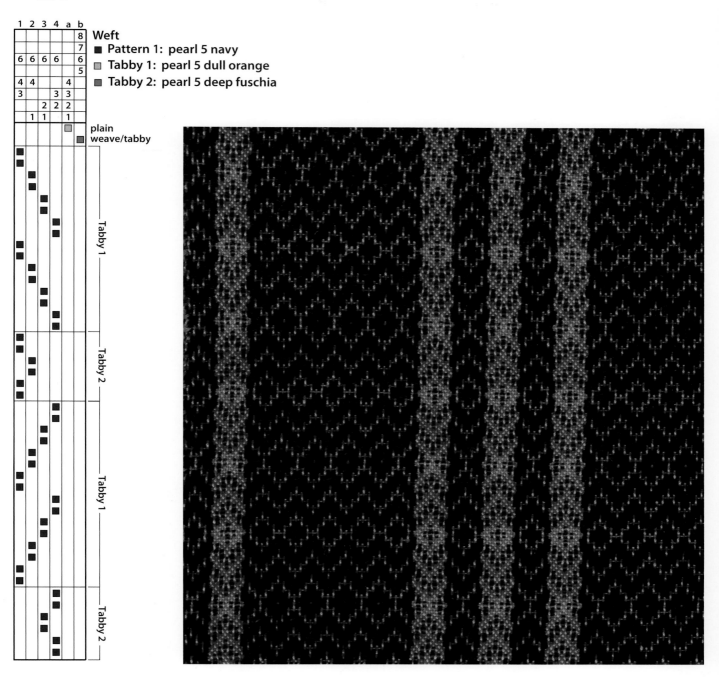

Weft
- ■ Pattern 1: pearl 5 navy
- ■ Tabby 1: pearl 5 dull orange
- ■ Tabby 2: pearl 5 deep fuschia

plain
weave/tabby

155-4

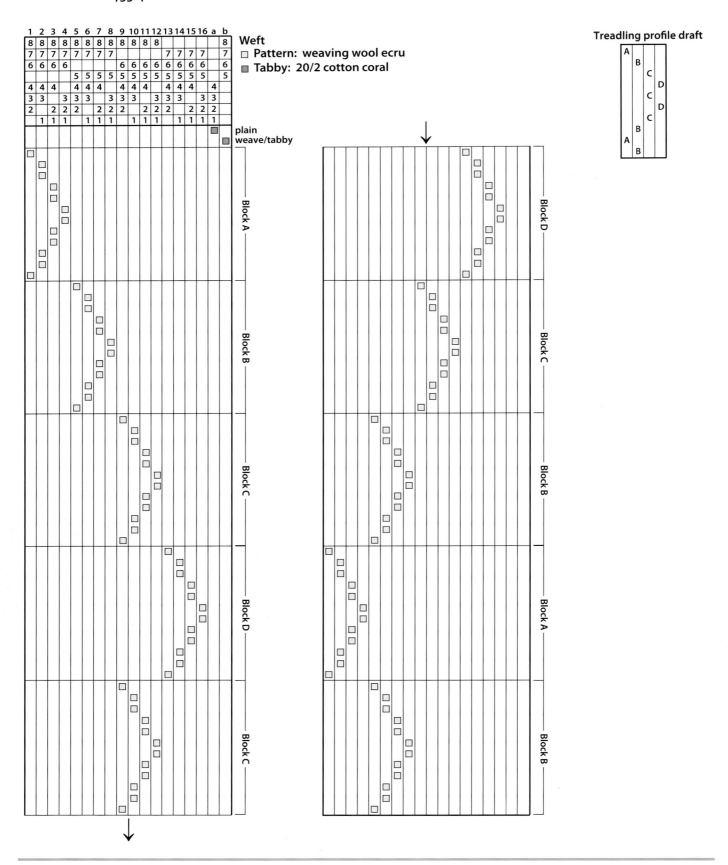

Weft
☐ Pattern: weaving wool ecru
▨ Tabby: 20/2 cotton coral

Treadling profile draft

Warp 158

Weave: Eight-shaft Single Four-tie
Sett: 30 epi
Warp: ☐ 20/2 Egyptian cotton natural

Threading block B

Threading block A

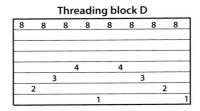

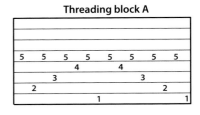

Threading block D

Threading block C

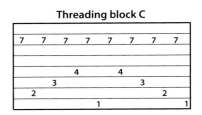

Threading profile draft

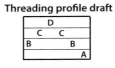

Threading repeat

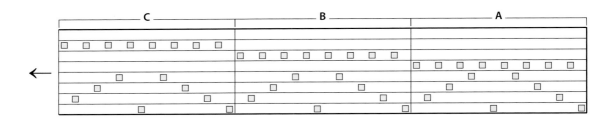

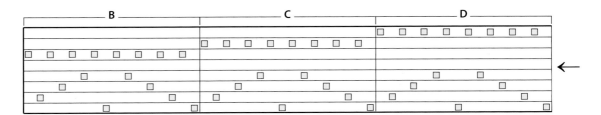

158-1

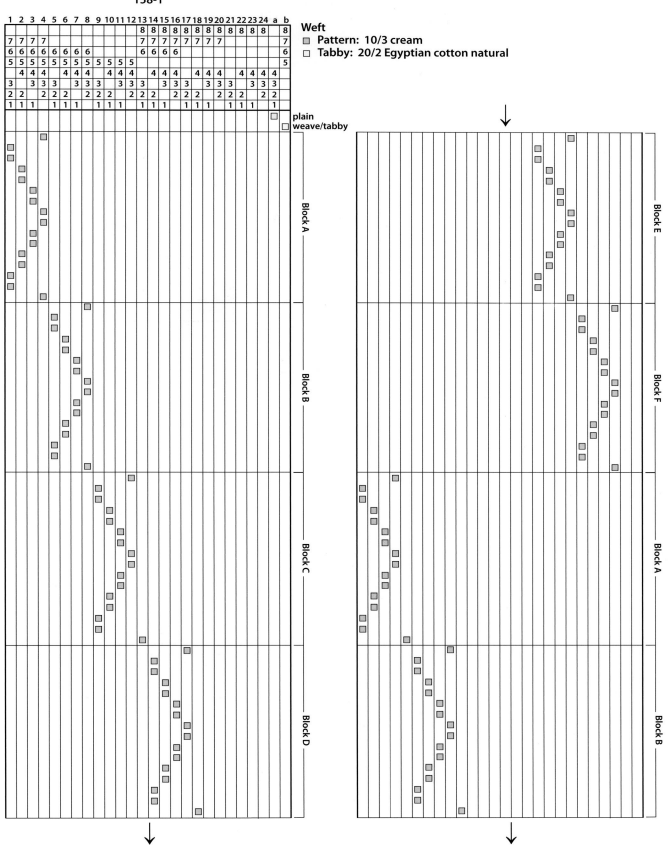

Weft
- Pattern: 10/3 cream
- Tabby: 20/2 Egyptian cotton natural

158-1 (continued)

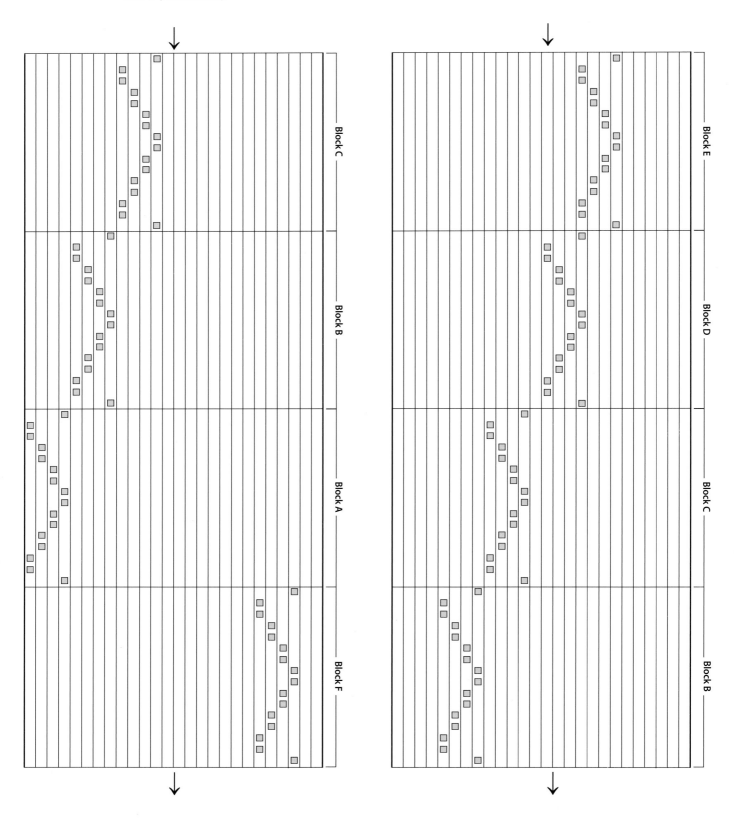

158-1 (continued)

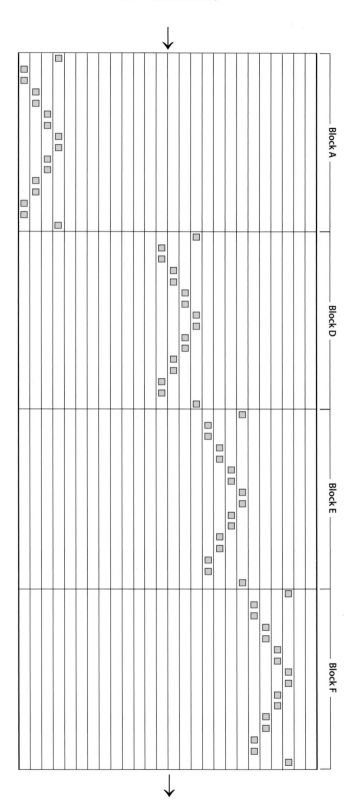

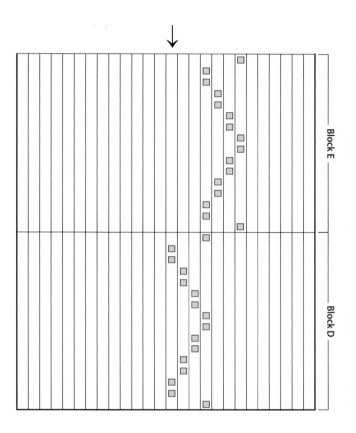

Treadling profile draft

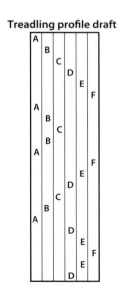

158-4

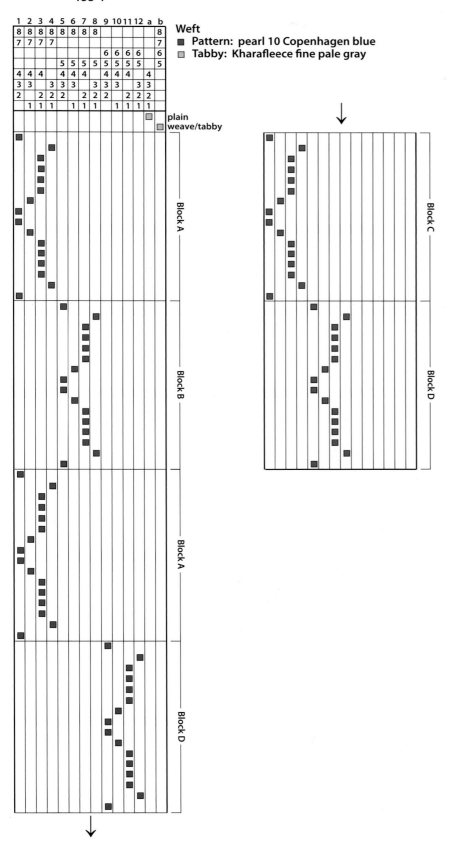

Weft

■ Pattern: pearl 10 Copenhagen blue
□ Tabby: Kharafleece fine pale gray

Treadling profile draft

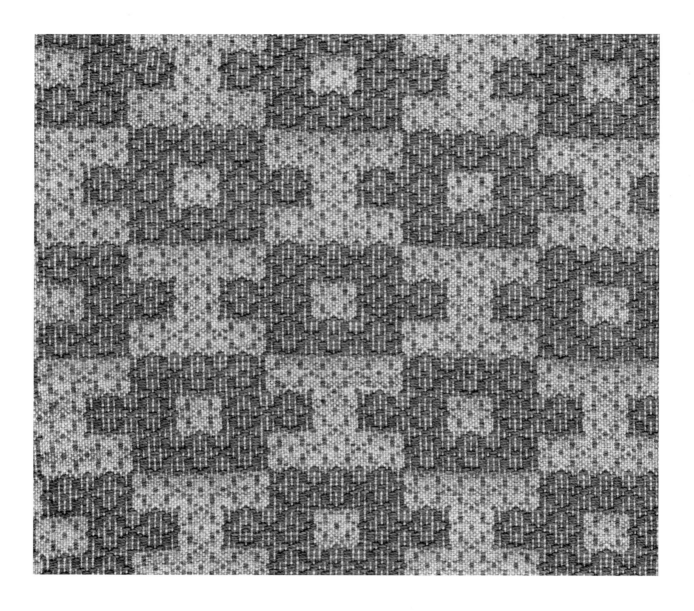

158-8

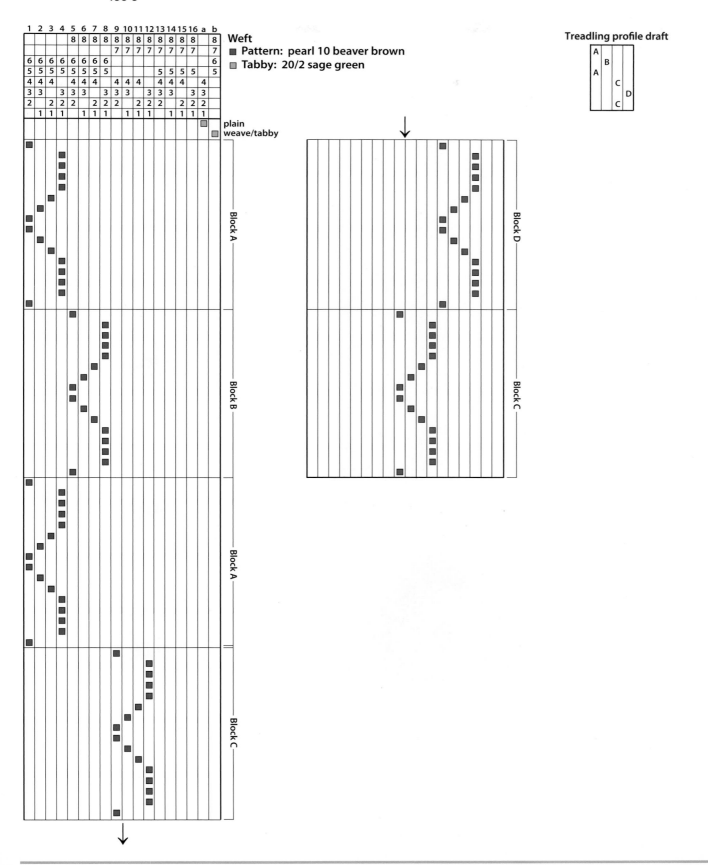

Treadling profile draft

Weft
- ■ Pattern: pearl 10 beaver brown
- ▢ Tabby: 20/2 sage green

plain weave/tabby

Block A

Block B

Block A

Block C

Block D

Block C

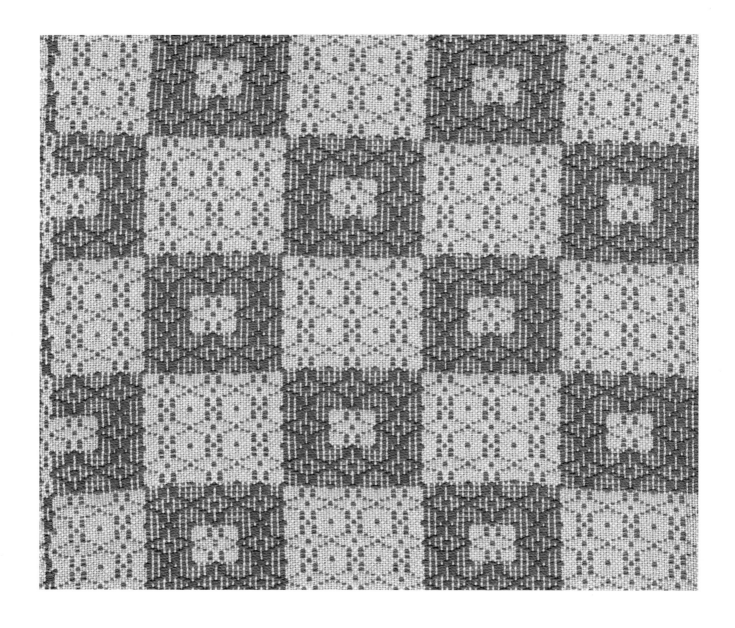

Warp 161

Weave: Eight-shaft Single Four-tie
Sett: 30 epi
Warp: ☐ 20/2 Egyptian cotton natural

Threading block B

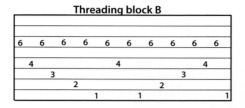

Threading block A

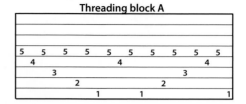

Threading block D

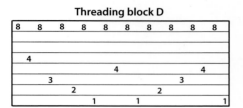

Threading block C

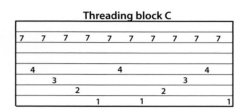

Threading profile draft

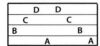

Threading repeat

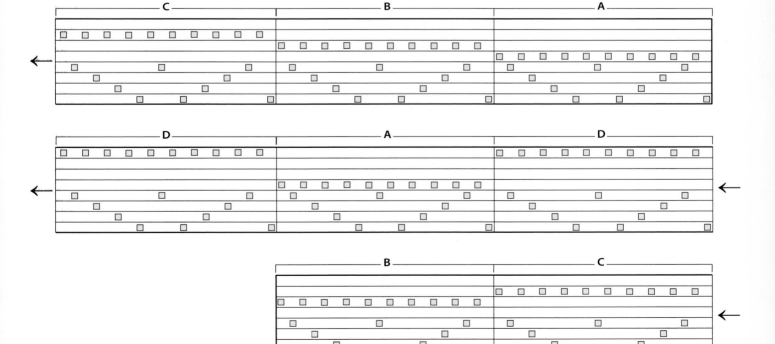

161-4

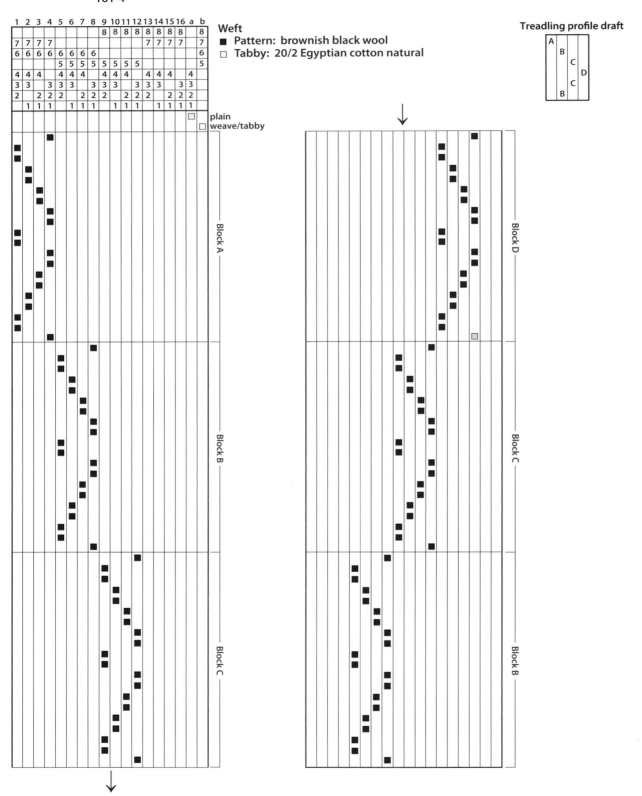

Weft

■ **Pattern: brownish black wool**
□ **Tabby: 20/2 Egyptian cotton natural**

Treadling profile draft

161-5

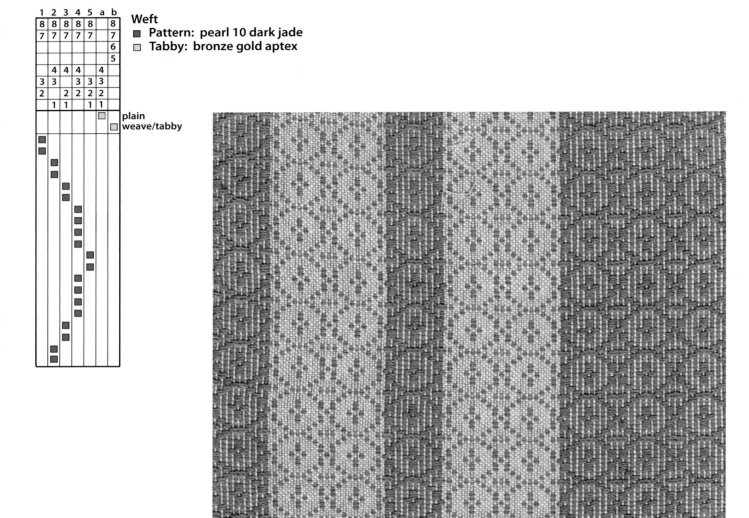

Weft

■ Pattern: pearl 10 dark jade

□ Tabby: bronze gold aptex

161-7

1	2	3	4	5	6	7	8	a	b
				8	8	8	8		8
7	7	7	7						7
6	6	6	6						6
				5	5	5	5		5
4	4			4	4				4
3			3	3			3	3	
		2	2			2	2	2	
	1	1			1	1		1	

Weft

- ■ **Pattern 1: pearl 10 lacquer**
- ▨ **Pattern 2: pearl 10 old gold**
- ▨ **Tabby: clove pink aptex**

Note: Due to the atypical tabby used for this sample, the weft picks for both the pattern and tabby are shown in the treadling sequence.

plain weave/tabby

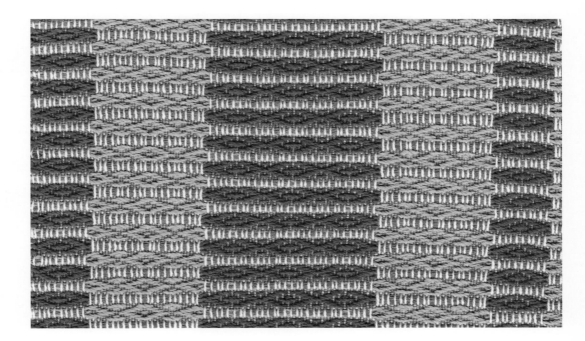

161-9

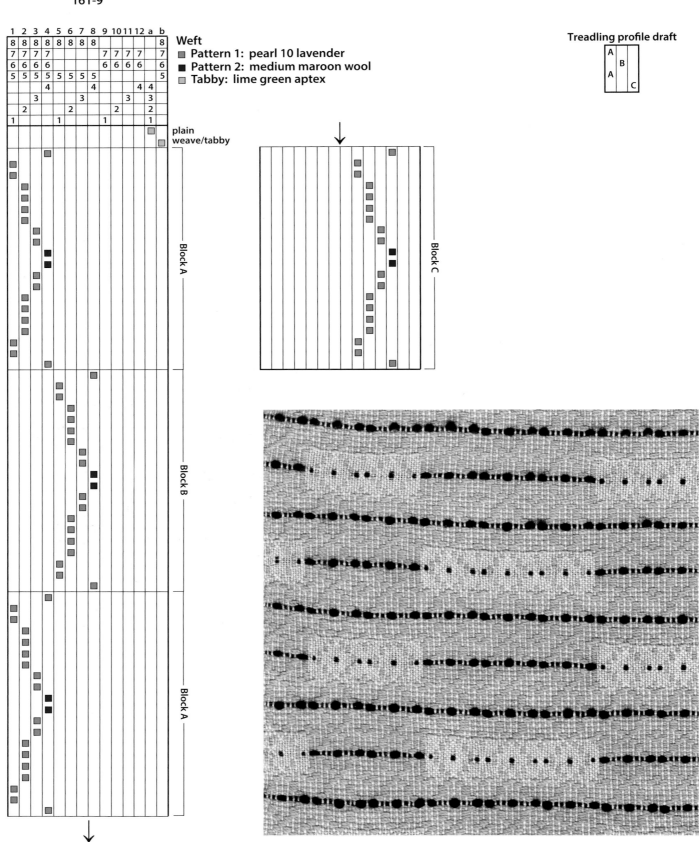

Weft
- Pattern 1: pearl 10 lavender
- Pattern 2: medium maroon wool
- Tabby: lime green aptex

plain weave/tabby

Block A

Block B

Block A

Block C

Treadling profile draft

A
A
B
C

161-10

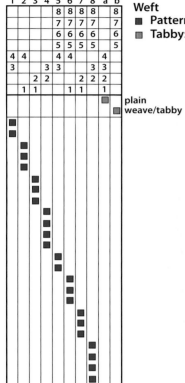

Weft
- ■ **Pattern: pearl 5 Peking blue**
- ▨ **Tabby: clove pink aptex**

plain
weave/tabby

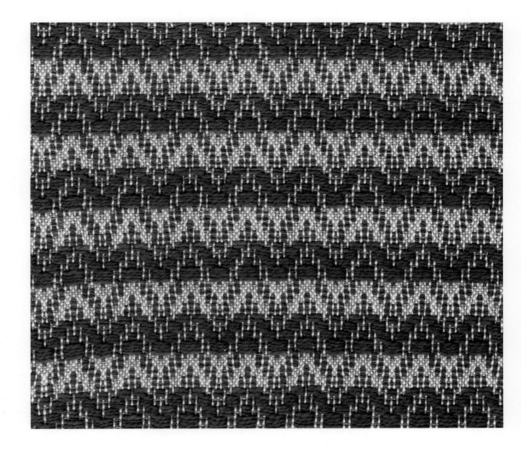

SECTION THREE
TWILL WEAVES

Dr. Bateman explored a variety of twill weaves; however, as with samples presented in earlier sections, he continued to vary tie-ups and treadling sequences, and produced some less-than-traditional interpretations. The samples presented in this section are examples of some of this work and are included in order to demonstrate the variety of weaves he studied.

In this section, each sample warp shows the following:

• Number assigned by Dr. Bateman
• Twill weave description
• Yarns and colors used for the warp ends
• Sett
• Complete threading repeat

For each sample, the following information is noted:

• Number and sub-number assigned by Dr. Bateman
• Yarns and colors used for weft picks
• Tie-up
• Plain weave and tabby treadles when applicable

Warp 143

Weave: Eight-shaft Twill
Sett: 22½ epi
Warp: ☐ 10/3 natural cotton

Threading repeat

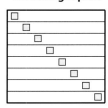

143-2

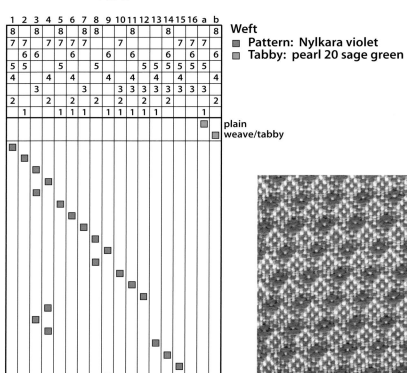

Weft
■ **Pattern:** Nylkara violet
■ **Tabby:** pearl 20 sage green

plain weave/tabby

Warp 277A

Weave: Six-shaft Twill
Sett: 30 epi
Warp: ■ pearl 20 bottle green

Threading repeat

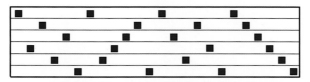

Note: Because of the threading sequence, a true plain weave for this threading is not possible.

277A-6

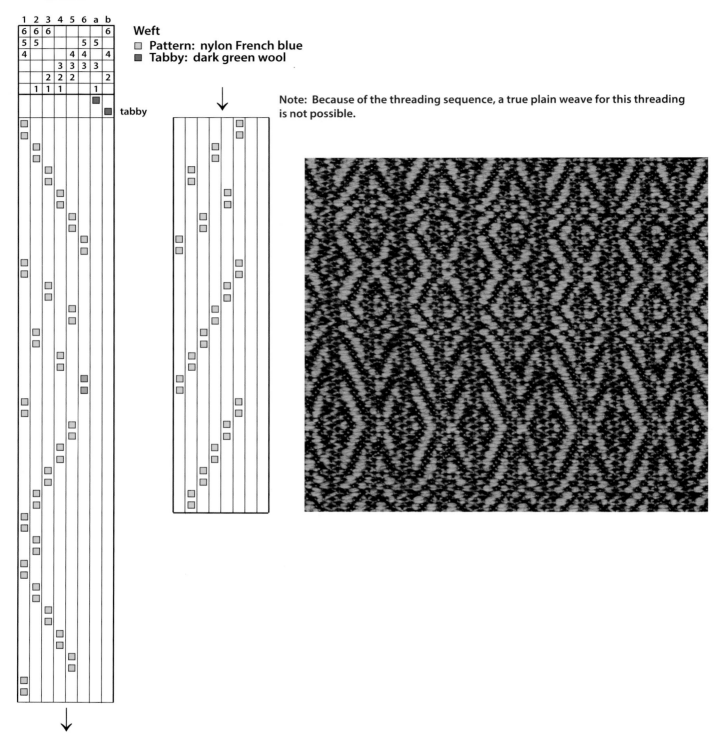

Weft
☐ Pattern: nylon French blue
■ Tabby: dark green wool

Note: Because of the threading sequence, a true plain weave for this threading is not possible.

277A-7

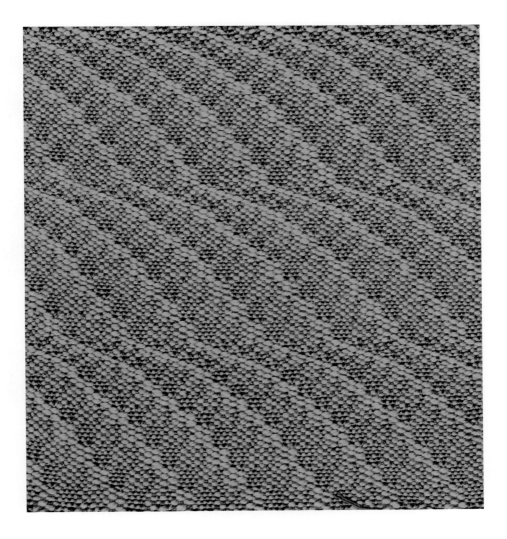

Weft

☐ Pattern: 10/3 cotton green

Note: Because of the threading sequence, a true plain weave for this threading is not possible.

Warp 282A

Weave: Eight-shaft Twill
Sett: 30 epi
Warp: □ 20/2 ecru

Threading repeat

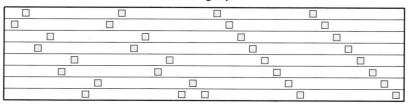

Note: Because of the threading sequence, a true plain weave for this threading is not possible.

282A-1

1	2	3	4	5	6	7	8	a	b
			8	8		8	8		8
7				7	7		7	7	
6	6				6	6			6
	5	5				5	5	5	
4		4	4				4		4
3	3		3	3				3	
	2	2		2	2				2
		1	1		1	1		1	

Weft
■ **Pattern:** dark green wool
□ **Tabby:** 50/3 light aqua

tabby

Note: Because of the threading sequence, a true plain weave for this threading is not possible.

282A-2

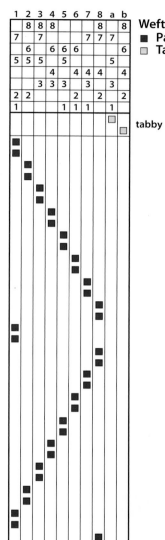

Weft
■ Pattern: pearl 5 rust
☐ Tabby: 20/1 ashes of roses

tabby

Note: Because of the threading sequence, a true plain weave for this threading is not possible.

282A-5

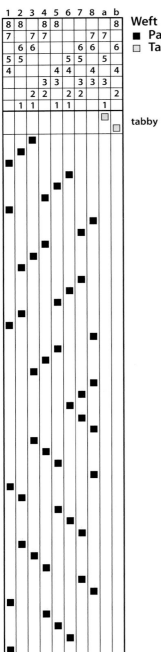

tabby

Weft
■ **Pattern:** black nylkara
□ **Tabby:** dull orange kharafleece

Note: Because of the threading sequence, a true plain weave for this threading is not possible.

Warp 285

Weave: Four-shaft Twill
Sett: 30 epi
Warp: ■ 20/2 cotton maroon

Threading repeat

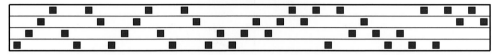

Note: Because of the threading sequence, a true plain weave for this threading
is not possible.

285 - 2

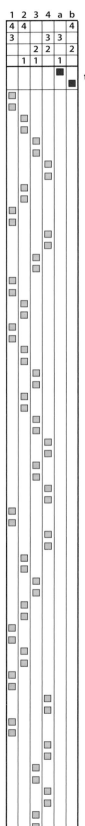

Weft

☐ **Pattern:** 10/3 cotton lavender
■ **Tabby:** 20/2 cotton maroon

Note: Because of the threading sequence, a true plain weave for this threading is not possible.

285 - 3

1	2	3	4	a	b
		4	4		4
	3	3			3
2	2				2
1			1	1	

Weft
■ Pattern: 10/3 rose fraise
■ Tabby: pearl 20 heliotrope

tabby

Note: Because of the threading sequence, a true plain weave for this threading is not possible.

285 - 4

1	2	3	4	a	b
		4	4		4
	3	3		3	
2	2				2
1			1	1	

tabby

Weft

☐ Pattern: Puritan crochet sky pink
☐ Tabby: Puritan crochet sky pink (same as Pattern weft)

Note: This sample is woven with a single alternating tabby. Because the order of the tabby picks is critical for the pattern to weave correctly, the tabby picks have been included in the treadling sequence. Also, because of the threading sequence, a true plain weave is not possible.

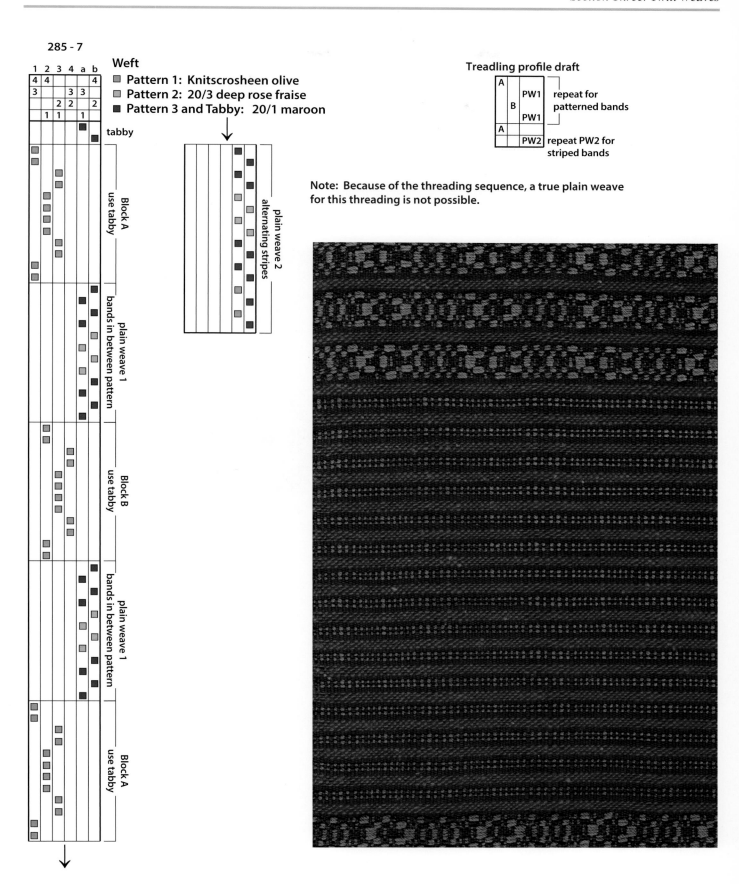

285 - 7

Weft

- ☐ Pattern 1: Knitscrosheen olive
- ☐ Pattern 2: 20/3 deep rose fraise
- ■ Pattern 3 and Tabby: 20/1 maroon

tabby

Block A
use tabby

plain weave 1
bands in between pattern

Block B
use tabby

plain weave 1
bands in between pattern

Block A
use tabby

plain weave 2
alternating stripes

Treadling profile draft

A			
	B	PW1	repeat for
		PW1	patterned bands
A			
		PW2	repeat PW2 for striped bands

Note: Because of the threading sequence, a true plain weave for this threading is not possible.

Warp 294

Weave: Eight-shaft Twill
Sett: 30 epi
Warp: □ 20/2 ecru

Threading repeat

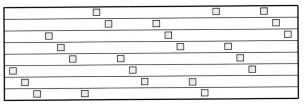

294-1

	1	2	3	4	5	6	7	8	a	b
	8	8			8	8				8
	7			7	7			7	7	
		6	6				6	6		6
	5	5				5	5		5	
	4			4	4			4	4	
			3	3			3	3	3	
		2	2			2	2			2
	1	1			1	1			1	

Weft

■ **Pattern: pearl 5 light rust**

□ **Tabby: pearl 20 dark ecru**

□ plain
□ weave/tabby

294-2

1	2	3	4	5	6	7	8	a	b
8	8	8				8			8
7	7			7			7	7	
6			6			6	6		6
		5			5	5	5	5	
	4			4	4	4			4
3			3	3	3			3	
		2	2	2			2		2
		1	1				1		1

Weft

■ **Pattern:** 10/3 navy
□ **Tabby:** 20/1 light terra cotta

□ plain
□ weave/tabby

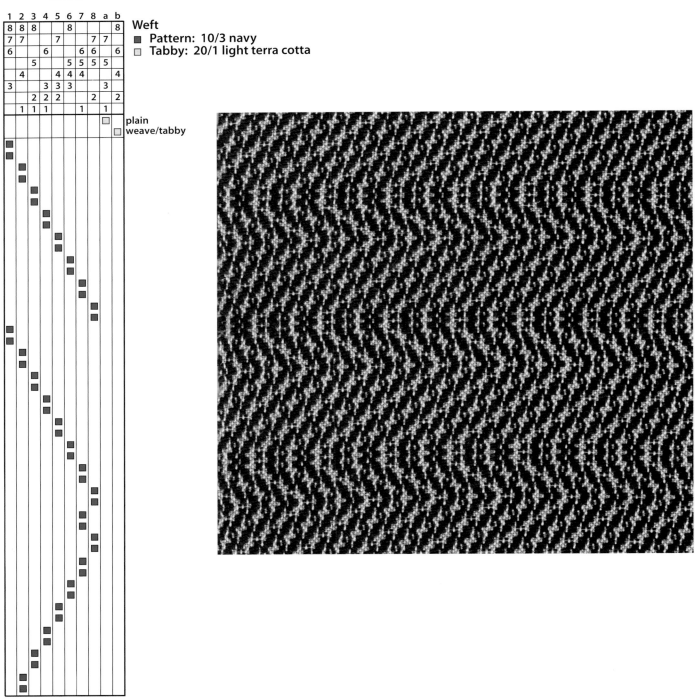

294-3

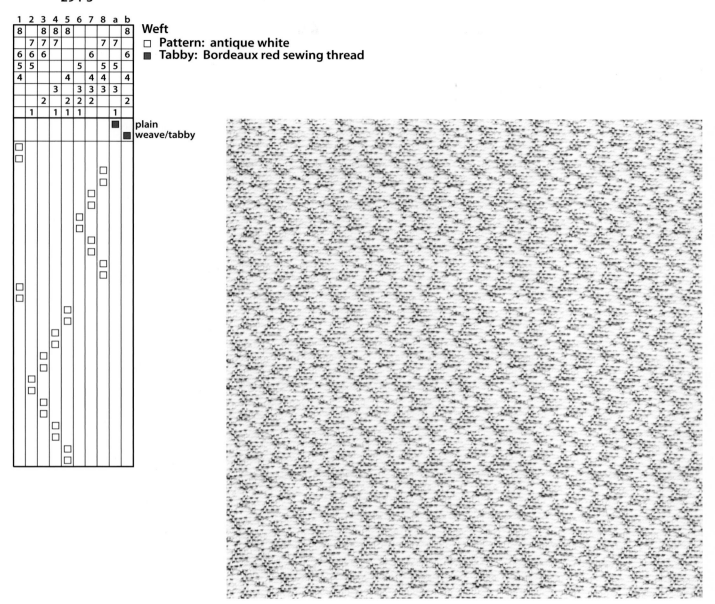

Weft
☐ **Pattern: antique white**
■ **Tabby: Bordeaux red sewing thread**

plain
weave/tabby

294-5

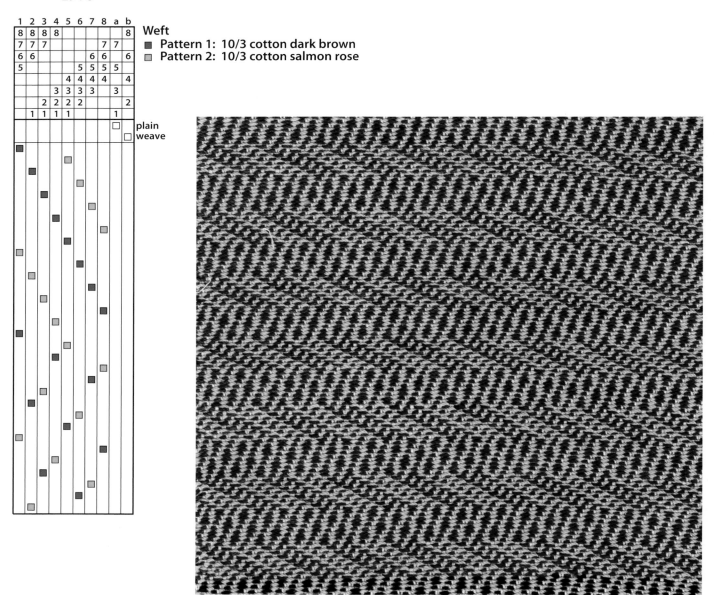

1	2	3	4	5	6	7	8	a	b
8	8	8	8						8
7	7	7					7	7	
6	6					6	6		6
5				5	5	5	5		
				4	4	4	4		4
			3	3	3	3		3	
		2	2	2	2				2
	1	1	1	1					1

□ plain
□ weave

Weft

■ **Pattern 1: 10/3 cotton dark brown**
□ **Pattern 2: 10/3 cotton salmon rose**

Warp 296

Weave: Six-shaft Twill

Sett: 30 epi

Warp: ☐ Star light rose beige

Threading repeat

296-1

Weft

■ **Pattern:** pearl 5 rust

☐ **Tabby:** Star light rose beige

☐ plain
☐ weave/tabby

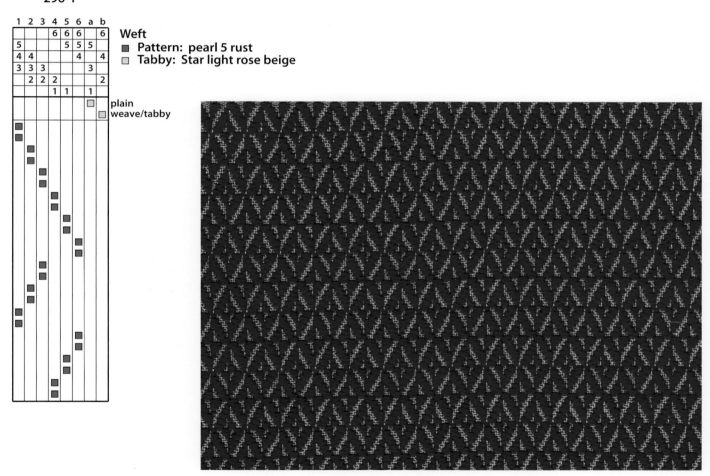

Warp 304

Weave: Six-shaft Twill

Sett: 30 epi

Warp: ☐ Arabian antique

Threading repeat

Note: Because of the threading sequence, a true plain weave for this threading is not possible.

304-2

Weft

■ **Pattern:** Bucilla royal blue

☐ **Tabby:** 24/2 ecru

Note: Because of the threading sequence, a true plain weave for this threading is not possible.

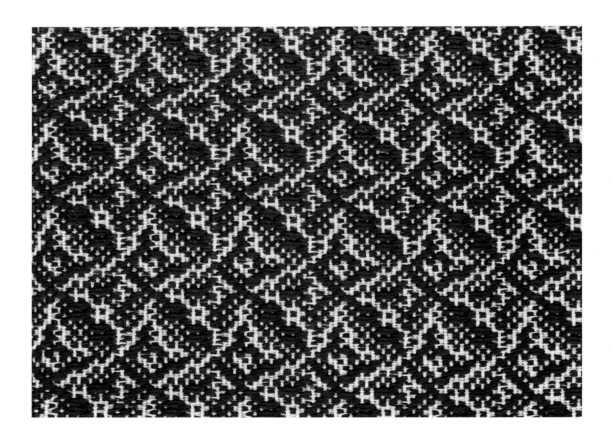

304-4

1	2	3	4	5	6	a	b
6	6		6				6
5		5			5	5	
		4			4	4		4
3			3	3			3
		2	2		2		2
	1	1		1		1	

Weft
■ **Pattern:** Carpet warp dark green
□ **Tabby:** grass green

tabby

Note: Because of the threading sequence, a true plain weave for this threading is not possible.

304-5

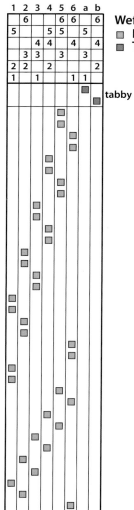

Weft
- Pattern: Carpet warp old rose
- Tabby: fine rayon dark pink

Note: Because of the threading sequence, a true plain weave for this threading is not possible.

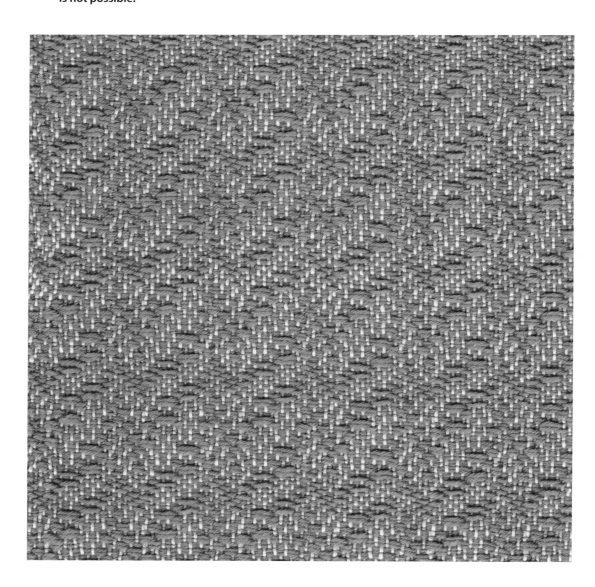

Warp 305

Weave: Eight-shaft Twill
Sett: 30 epi
Warp: ☐ carpet warp ecru
  ■ carpet warp brown

Threading repeat

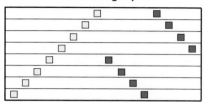

Note: Because of the threading sequence, a true plain weave for this threading is not possible.

305-1

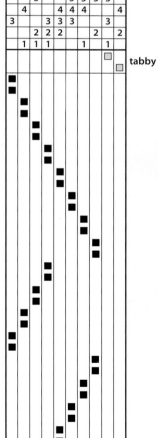

Weft
■ Pattern: Carpet warp black
☐ Tabby: 24/2 ecru

Note: Because of the threading sequence, a true plain weave for this threading is not possible.

305-2

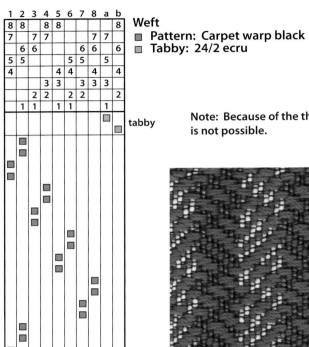

Weft
- ☐ Pattern: Carpet warp black
- ☐ Tabby: 24/2 ecru

tabby

Note: Because of the threading sequence, a true plain weave for this threading is not possible.

305-4

1	2	3	4	5	6	7	8	a	b
			8		8	8	8		8
	7			7	7	7		7	
		6		6	6	6			6
5		5	5	5					5
	4	4	4				4		4
3	3	3				3		3	
2	2			2		2		2	
1			1		1	1	1		

tabby

Weft
☐ **Pattern:** Carpet warp turquoise
☐ **Tabby:** Carpet warp turquoise (same as pattern weft)

Note: Because of the threading sequence, a true plain weave for this threading
is not possible.

Warp 306

Weave: Four-shaft Twill
Sett: 15 epi
Warp: ☐ 10/3 gray

Threading repeat

306-1

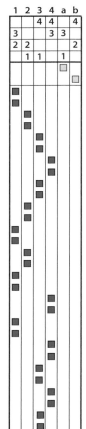

Weft
■ Pattern: Spanish tile wool
☐ Tabby: pearl 20 dark ecru

plain
☐ weave/tabby

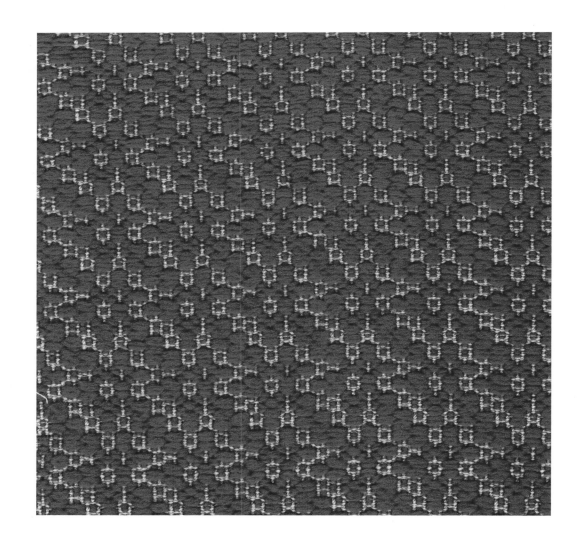

306-6

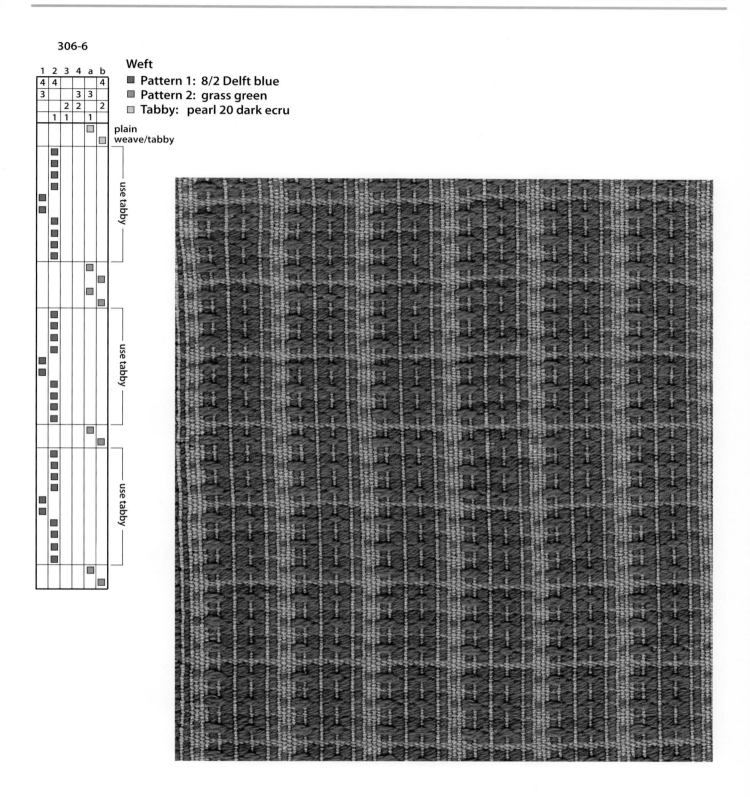

Weft

■ Pattern 1: 8/2 Delft blue
■ Pattern 2: grass green
□ Tabby: pearl 20 dark ecru

Warp 329

Weave: Four-shaft Twill

Sett: 30 epi

Warp 1: ■ **20/2 coral**

Warp 2: □ **Bernat Umbrian ecru**

Threading repeat

329-1

1	2	3	4	a	b
		4	4		4
3			3	3	
2	2				2
		1	1		1

plain
weave/tabby

Weft

■ Pattern: wine weaving wool

□ Tabby: pearl 20 dark ecru

329-3

1	2	3	4	a	b
		4	4		4
	3	3		3	
2	2				2
1			1	1	

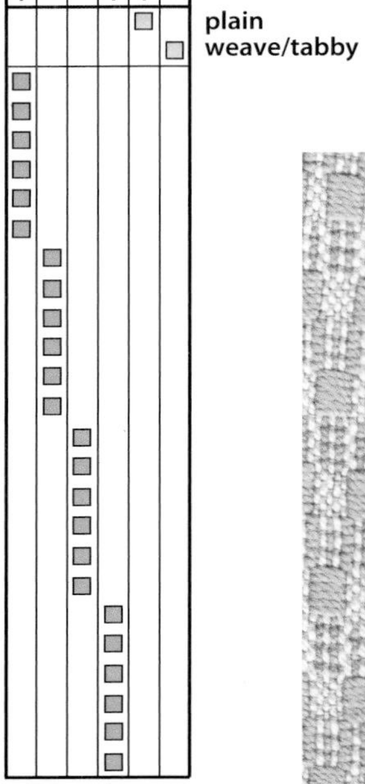

Weft
- ▣ Pattern: 10/2 salmon rose
- ☐ Tabby: 50/3 rose beige

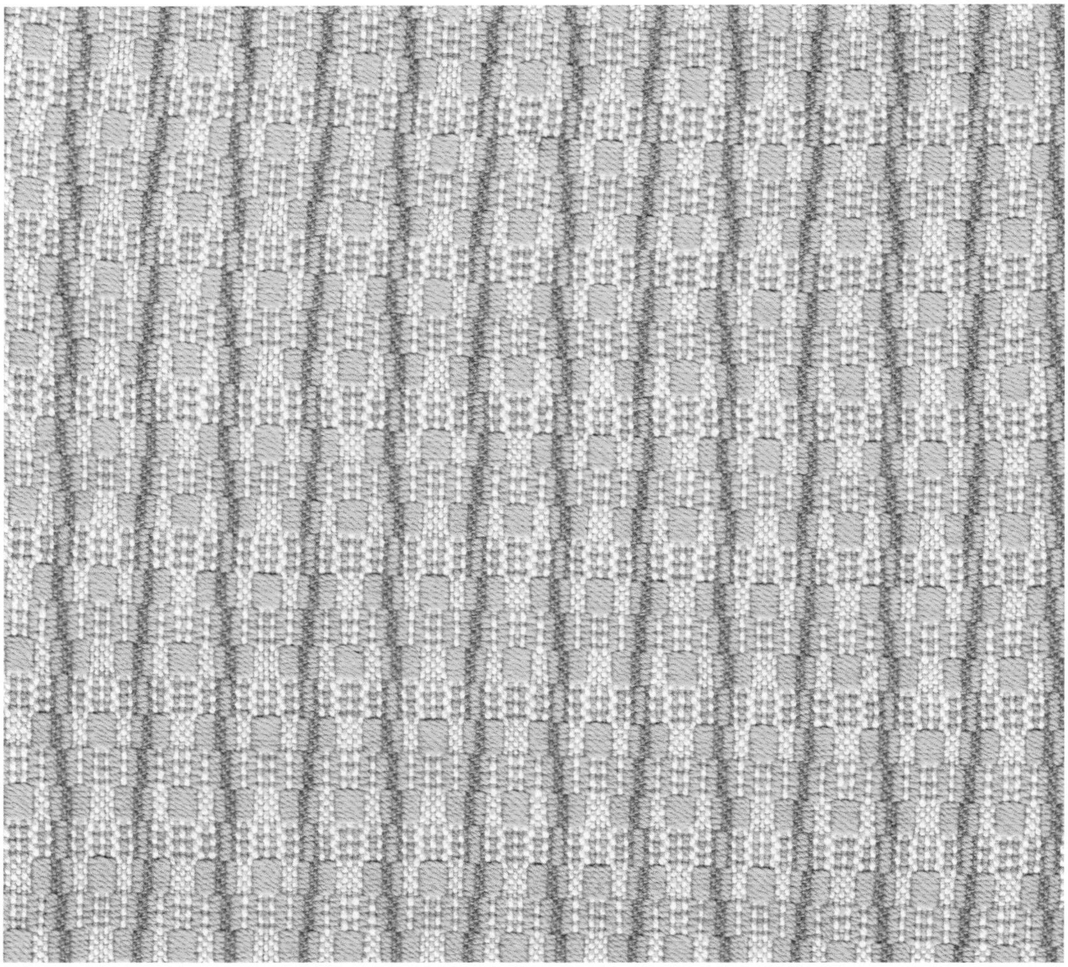

plain weave/tabby

Warp 373

Weave: Eight-shaft Twill
Sett: 30 epi
Warp: ▫ Bernat Umbrian medium burnt orange

Threading repeat

Note: Because of the threading sequence, a true plain weave for this threading is not possible.

373-1

1	2	3	4	5	6	7	8
8	8	8			8		
7	7			7			7
6			6			6	6
		5			5	5	5
	4			4	4	4	
3			3	3	3		
		2	2	2			2
	1	1	1			1	

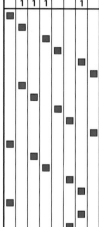

Weft
■ Pattern: pearl 5 rust

Note: Because of the threading sequence, a true plain weave for this threading is not possible.

373-5

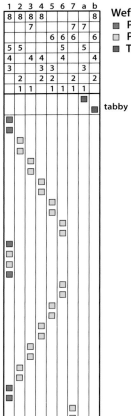

Weft

- ■ **Pattern 1:** Delft blue
- □ **Pattern 2:** yellow
- ■ **Tabby:** 10/3 bottle green

Note: Because of the threading sequence, a true plain weave for this threading is not possible.

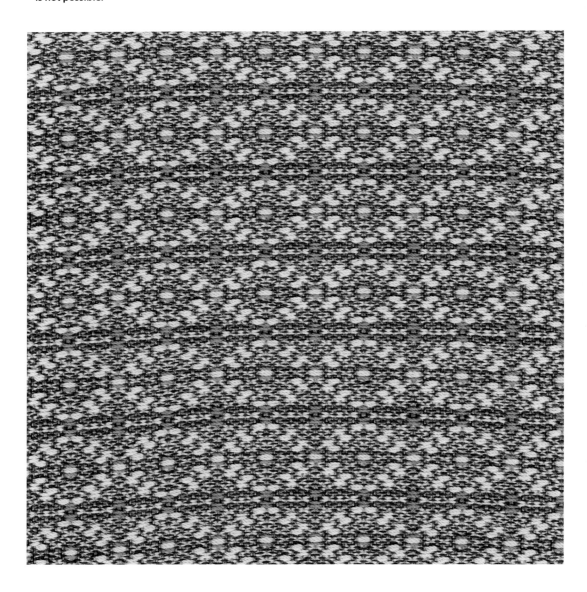

Warp 380

Weave: Eight-shaft Twill
Sett: 30 epi
Warp: ☐ 20/2 ecru

Threading repeat

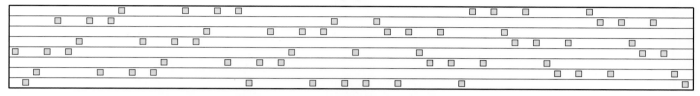

Note: Because of the threading sequence, a true plain weave for this threading is not possible.

380-1

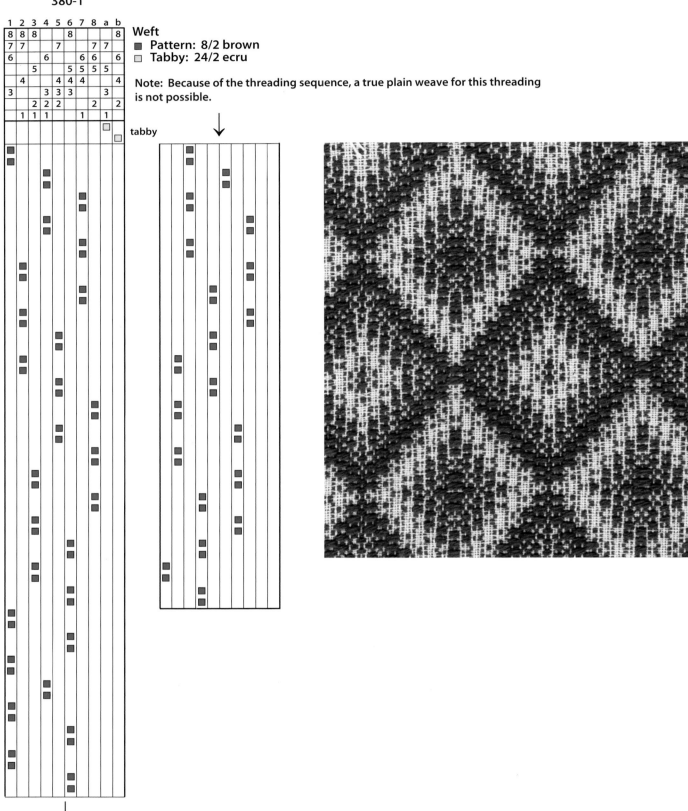

1	2	3	4	5	6	7	8	a	b
8	8	8				8			8
7	7				7		7	7	
6			6			6	6		6
		5			5	5	5	5	
	4			4	4	4			4
3			3	3	3			3	
		2	2	2			2		2
	1	1	1			1		1	

Weft
- ■ Pattern: 8/2 brown
- ☐ Tabby: 24/2 ecru

Note: Because of the threading sequence, a true plain weave for this threading is not possible.

tabby

380-2

	1	2	3	4	5	6	7	8	a	b
	8	8			8	8				8
	7			7	7				7	7
		6	6				6	6		6
	5	5				5	5			5
	4			4	4			4		4
			3	3			3	3	3	
		2	2			2	2			2
		1	1			1	1			1

Weft

- ■ Pattern: 6 strand filler greenish blue
- ▢ Tabby: 50/3 aqua

Note: Because of the threading sequence, a true plain weave for this threading is not possible.

tabby

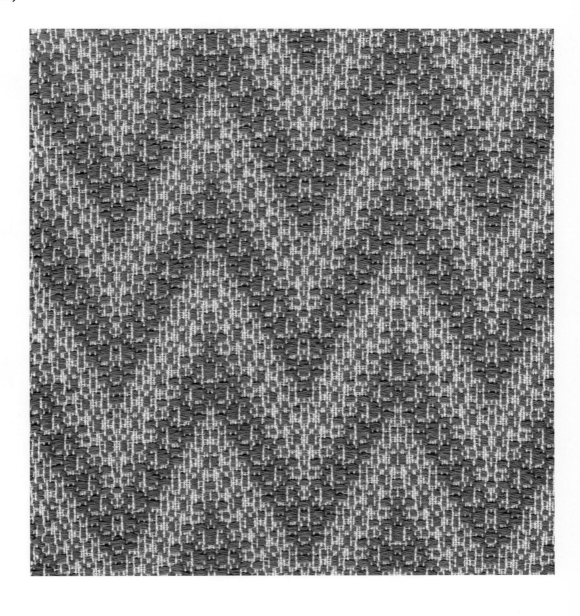

380-4

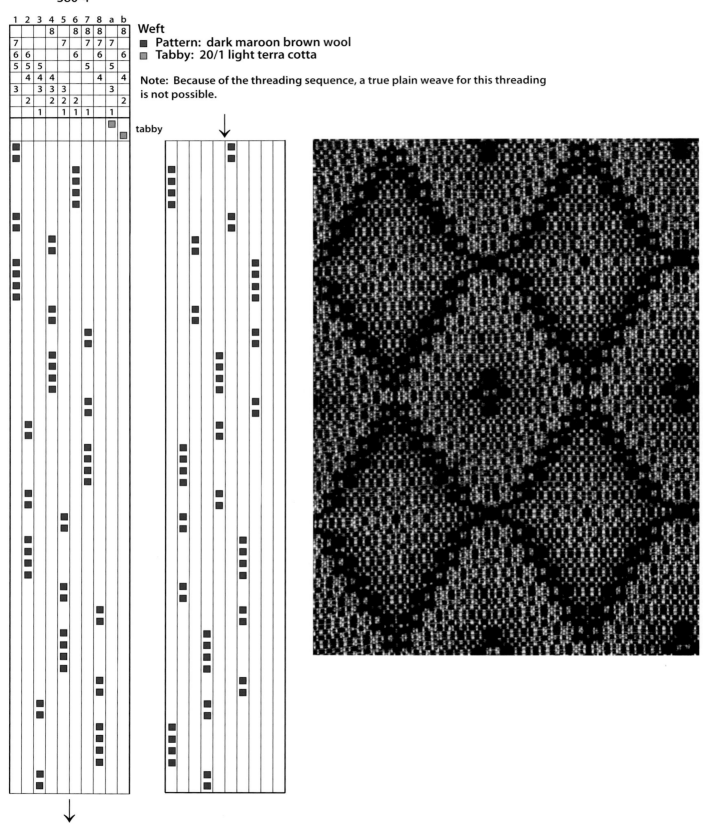

Weft
- ■ Pattern: dark maroon brown wool
- ▪ Tabby: 20/1 light terra cotta

Note: Because of the threading sequence, a true plain weave for this threading is not possible.

tabby

SECTION FOUR
OTHER WEAVES

Dr. Bateman explored a variety of traditional weaves; however, as with samples presented in earlier sections, he continued to vary tie-ups and treadling sequences, and produced some less-than-traditional interpretations. The samples presented in this section are examples of some of this work and are included in order to demonstrate the variety of weaves he studied.

In this section, each sample warp shows the following:

• Number assigned by Dr. Bateman
• Weave description
• Yarns and colors used for the warp ends
• Sett
• Complete threading repeat

For each sample, the following information is noted:

• Number and sub-number assigned by Dr. Bateman
• Yarns and colors used for weft picks
• Tie-up
• Plain weave and tabby treadles when applicable

Warp 354

Weave: Six-shaft Crackle

Sett: 30 epi

Warp: □ #40 crochet cotton white

Threading repeat

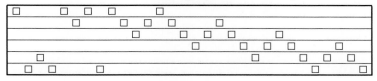

354-1

1	2	3	4	5	6	a	b
6	6				6		6
	5	5				5	5
4		4	4				4
	3		3	3			3
		2		2	2		2
1			1		1	1	

Weft

■ Pattern: 10/3 red

□ Tabby: #40 crochet cotton white

□ plain
□ weave/tabby

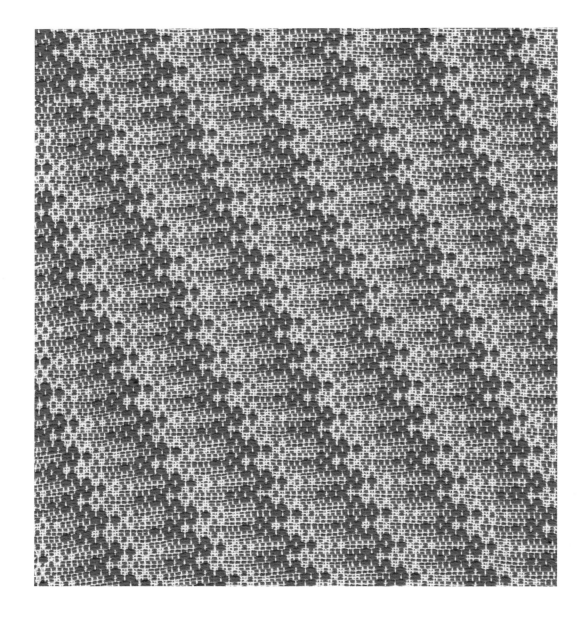

354-2

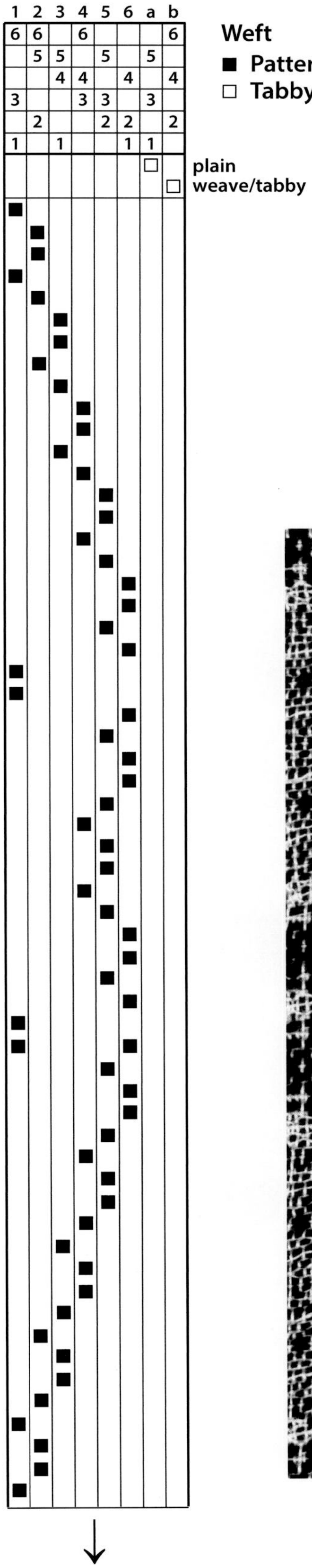

Weft

■ Pattern: carpet warp black

□ Tabby: #40 crochet cotton white

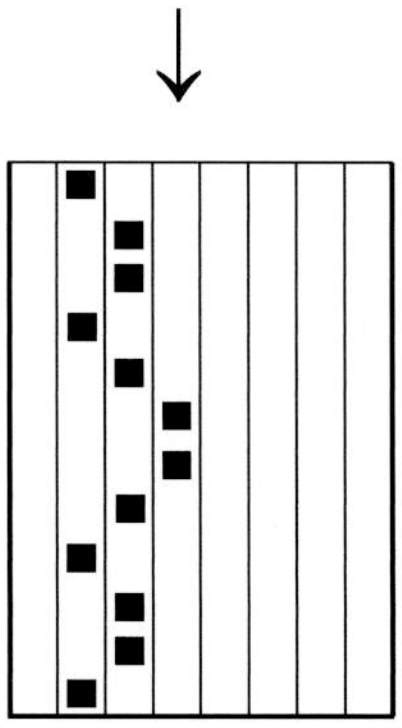

□ plain
□ weave/tabby

354-3

1	2	3	4	5	6	a	b
			6	6		6	6
5			5	5		5	
	4			4	4		4
3		3			3	3	
2	2		2				2
	1	1		1		1	

☐ plain
☐ weave/tabby

Weft
☐ **Pattern 1:** 10/3 ecru
☐ **Pattern 2:** 10/3 light blue
▨ **Pattern 3:** 10/3 turquoise
▨ **Pattern 4:** 10/3 delft blue
■ **Pattern 5:** 10/3 skipper blue
■ **Pattern 6:** 10/3 navy
☐ **Tabby:** #40 crochet cotton white

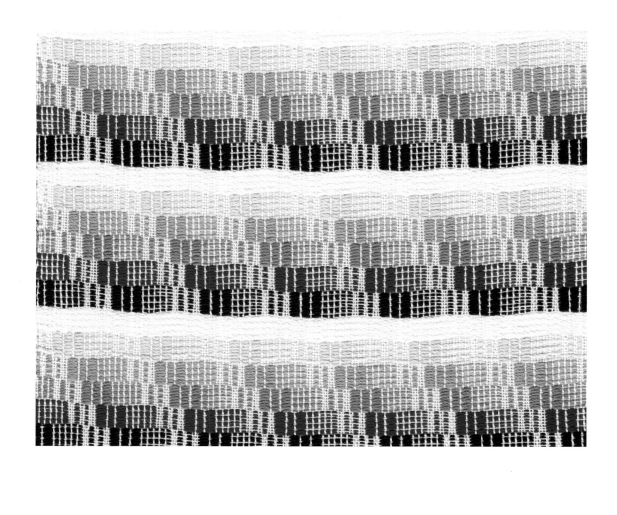

354-4

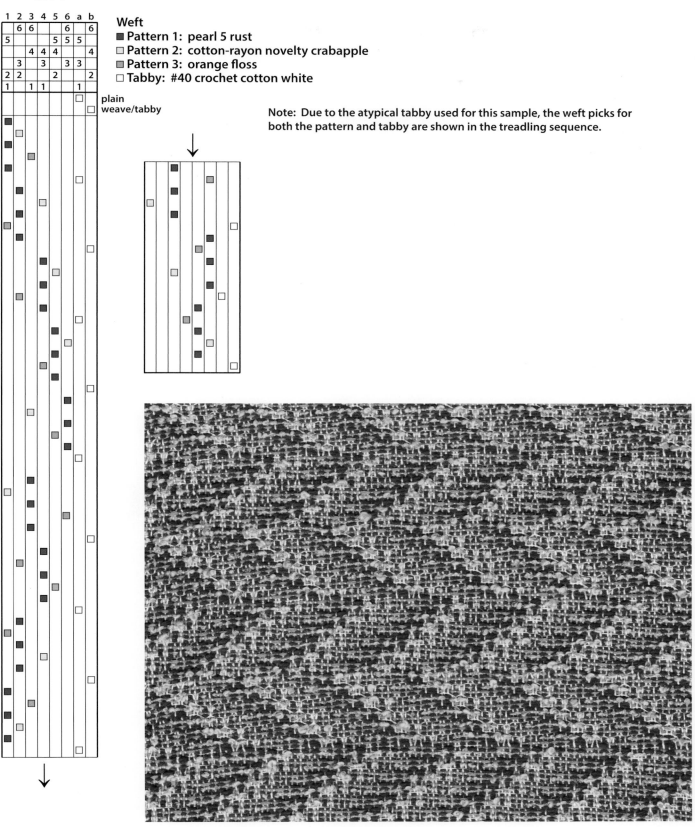

Weft
■ Pattern 1: pearl 5 rust
□ Pattern 2: cotton-rayon novelty crabapple
■ Pattern 3: orange floss
□ Tabby: #40 crochet cotton white

plain weave/tabby

Note: Due to the atypical tabby used for this sample, the weft picks for both the pattern and tabby are shown in the treadling sequence.

Warp 356

Weave: Six-shaft Crackle
Sett: 30 epi
Warp: ■ Bernats umbrian flame

Threading repeat

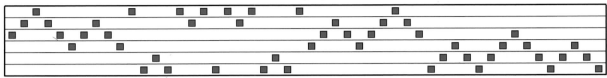

356-1

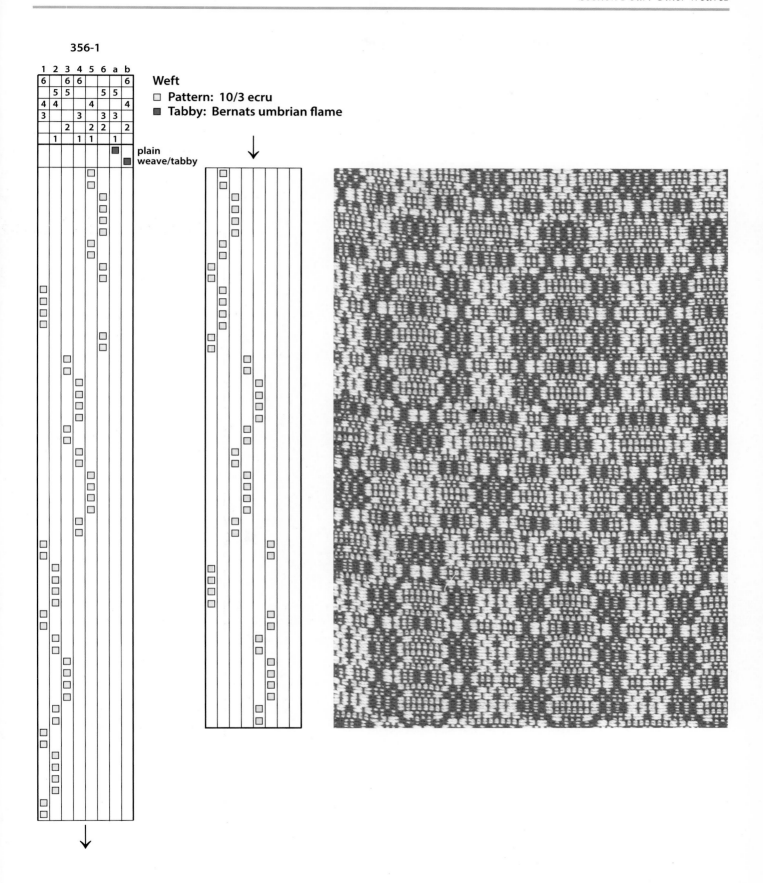

Weft

☐ **Pattern: 10/3 ecru**

■ **Tabby: Bernats umbrian flame**

plain
weave/tabby

356-2

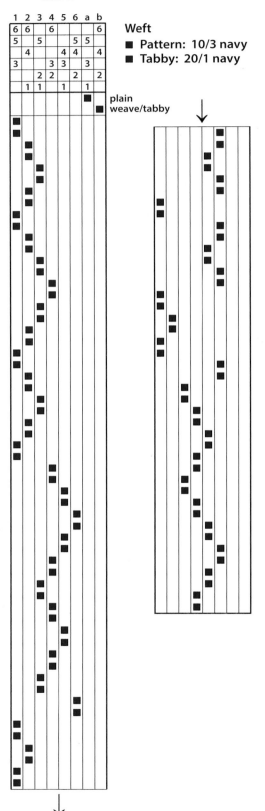

Weft
- ■ Pattern: 10/3 navy
- ■ Tabby: 20/1 navy

Warp 259 and 259A

Weave: Four-shaft Overshot
Sett: 30 epi
Warp: ☐ pearl 20 natural

Threading repeat

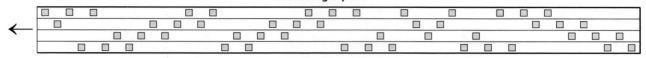

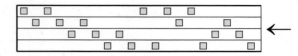

259-1

1	2	3	4	a	b
4	4				4
3			3	3	
		2	2	2	
	1	1		1	

plain
weave/tabby

Weft

□ Pattern: pearl 5 dark brown
□ Tabby: pearl 20 natural

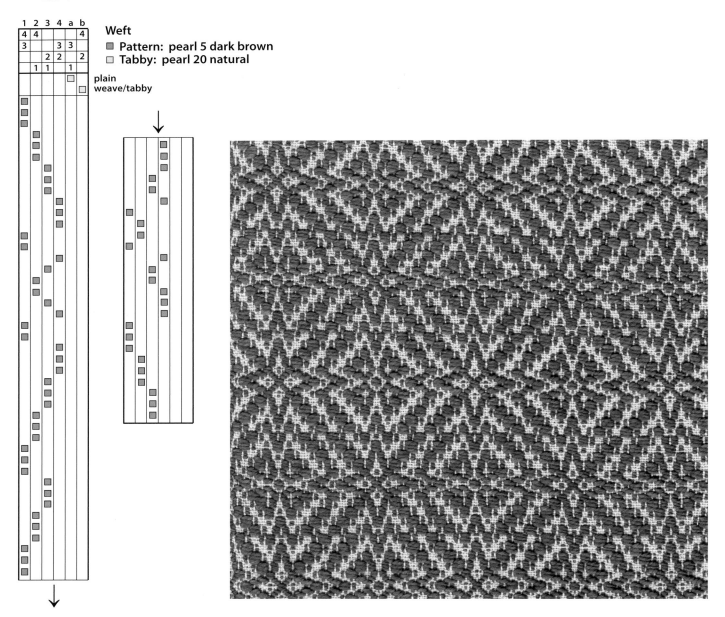

259-7

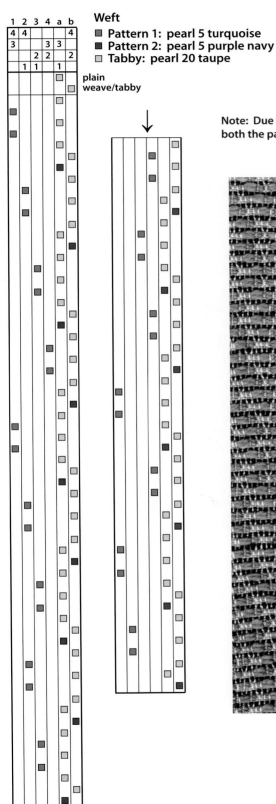

Weft

- ■ Pattern 1: pearl 5 turquoise
- ■ Pattern 2: pearl 5 purple navy
- □ Tabby: pearl 20 taupe

plain
weave/tabby

Note: Due to the atypical tabby used for this sample, the weft picks for both the pattern and tabby are shown in the treadling sequence.

259A-7

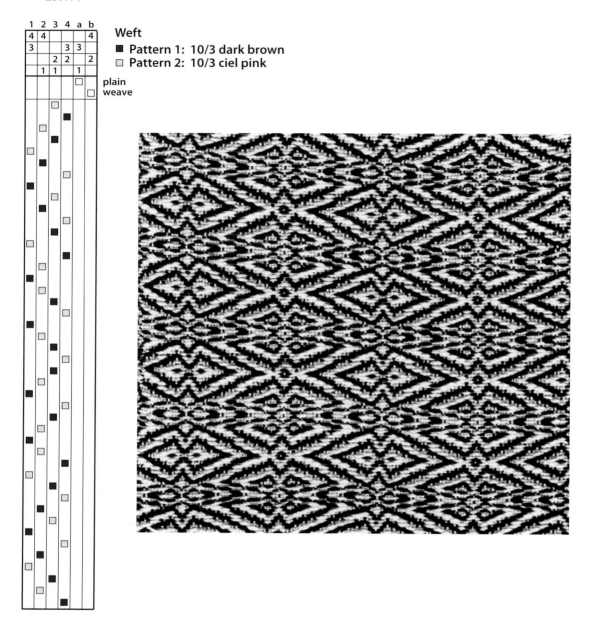

Weft
- ■ Pattern 1: 10/3 dark brown
- □ Pattern 2: 10/3 ciel pink

plain weave

Warp 317

Weave: Eight-shaft Overshot
Sett: 30 epi
Warp: □ pearl 20 ecru

Threading repeat

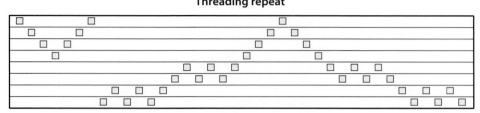

317-1

Weft
- ▪ **Pattern: pearl 5 rust**
- ▫ **Tabby: pearl 20 buff**

plain
weave/tabby

317-4

1	2	3	4	5	6	7	8	a	b
		8	8	8	8	8			8
7			7	7	7		7	7	
6	6			6		6	6		6
	5	5			5	5		5	
		4	4	4	4				4
3			3	3			3	3	
2	2					2	2		2
	1	1			1	1	1	1	

Weft
- ■ Pattern: weaving wool dark green
- ▨ Tabby: pearl 20 pistachio

▨ plain weave/tabby

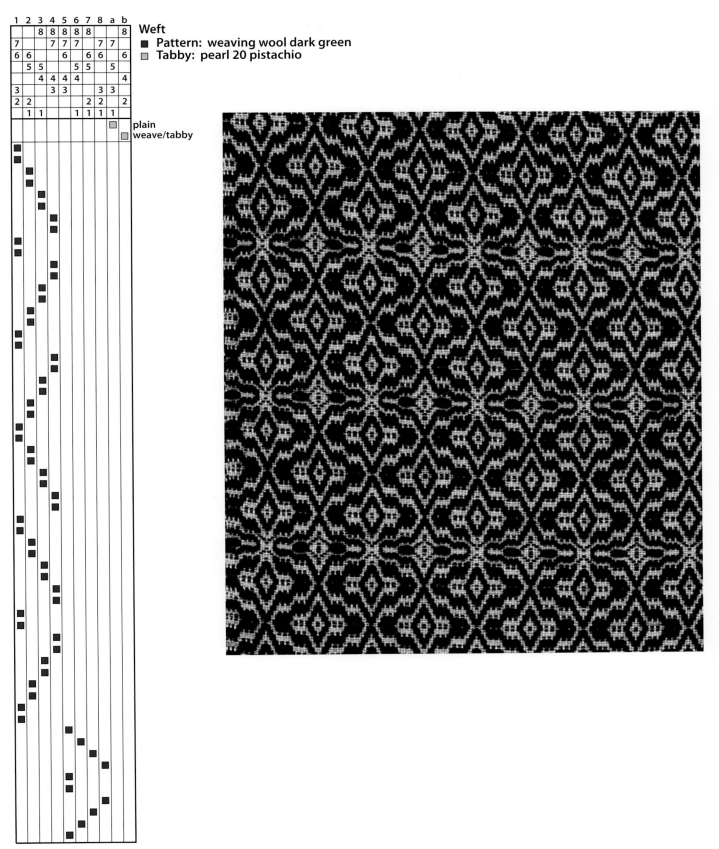

317-6

	1	2	3	4	5	6	7	8	a	b
	8	8		8	8					8
	7		7	7				7	7	
		6	6			6	6		6	
	5	5			5	5		5		
	4			4	4		4		4	
			3	3		3	3	3		
		2	2		2	2			2	
	1	1		1	1			1		

Weft
■ **Pattern:** maroon wool
□ **Tabby:** 50/3 rose beige

□ plain
□ weave/tabby

Warp 321

Weave: Eight-shaft Overshot
Sett: 30 epi
Warp: ■ Delph blue crochet cotton

Threading repeat

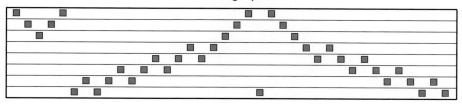

321-1

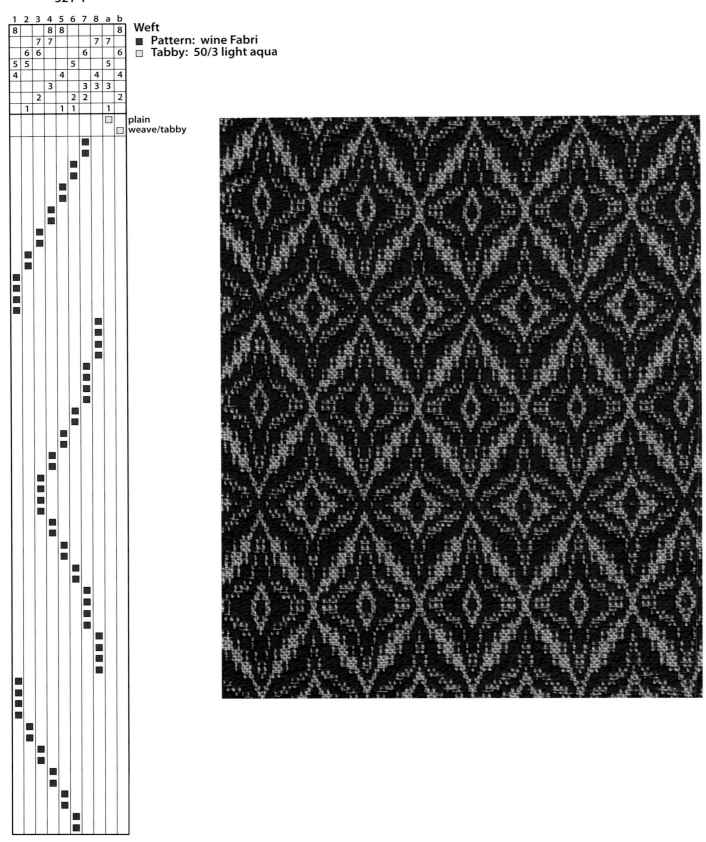

Weft
- ■ **Pattern:** wine Fabri
- □ **Tabby:** 50/3 light aqua

□ plain
□ weave/tabby

321-2

1	2	3	4	5	6	7	8	a	b
8	8	8			8				8
7	7			7			7	7	
6			6			6	6		6
		5			5	5	5	5	
	4			4	4	4			4
3			3	3	3			3	
		2	2	2			2		2
	1	1	1				1		1

Weft
- ■ Pattern: red-purple wool
- ■ Tabby: 50/3 raspberry rose

■ plain
■ weave/tabby

321-3

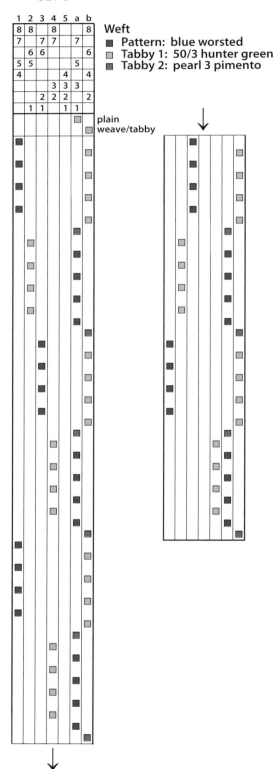

Weft

- ■ Pattern: blue worsted
- □ Tabby 1: 50/3 hunter green
- ■ Tabby 2: pearl 3 pimento

□ plain
  weave/tabby

Note: Due to the atypical tabby used for this sample, the weft picks for both the pattern and tabby are shown in the treadling sequence.

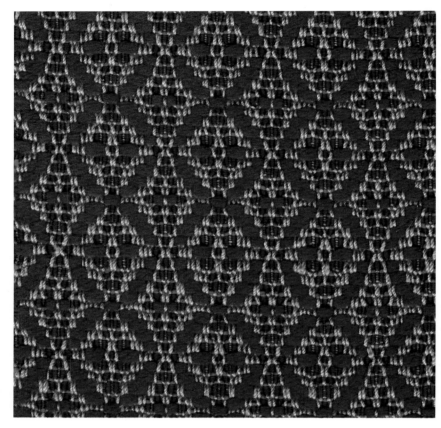

321-4

1	2	3	4	5	6	7	8	a	b
8	8		8	8					8
7		7	7			7	7		
	6	6			6	6			6
5	5			5	5		5		
4			4	4		4			4
		3	3		3	3	3		
	2	2		2	2				2
	1	1		1	1			1	

Weft

☐ Pattern 1: weaving wool peach
■ Pattern 2: weaving wool black
☐ Tabby: 50/3 rose beige

☐ plain weave/tabby

Warp 322

Weave: Four-shaft Overshot
Sett: approximately 24 epi (see warp information below)
Warp 1: ☐ delph blue crochet cotton on shaft four (1 per dent in 15-dent reed)
Warp 2: ☐ 10/3 cotton yellow on shaft three (1 per dent in 15-dent reed)
Warp 3: ☐ 20/2 cotton ecru on shafts one and two (2 per dent in 15-dent reed)

Threading repeat

322-1

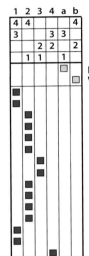

Weft
■ **Pattern:** 10/3 cotton skipper blue
☐ **Tabby:** 50/3 gray beige

plain
weave/tabby

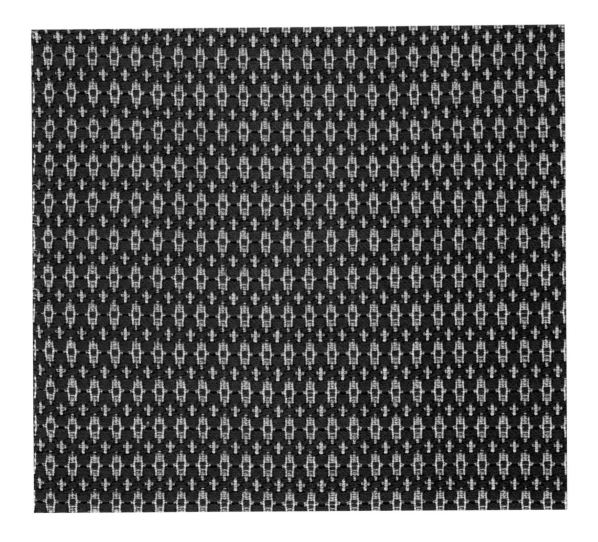

322-2

Weft
- ☐ Pattern 1: Bucilla orange-gold
- ◼ Pattern 2: Bucilla medium rust
- ☐ Tabby: 50/3 deep beige

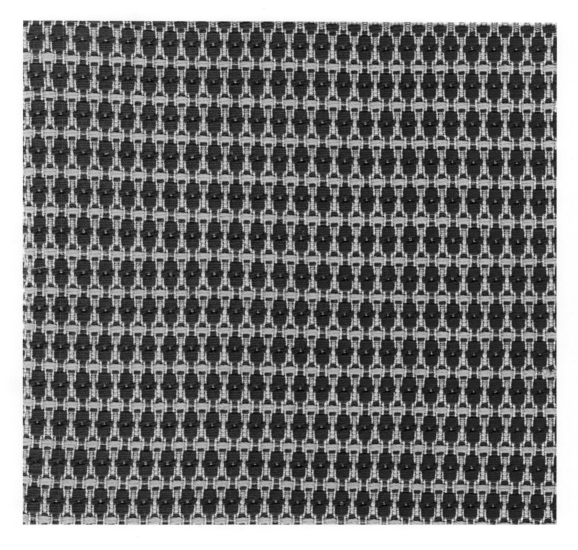

322-4

Weft

- ■ **Pattern 1:** pearl 5 peacock blue
- ■ **Pattern 2:** pearl 3 black
- □ **Tabby:** pearl 20 aqua

Note: Due to the atypical tabby used for this sample, the weft picks for both the pattern and tabby are shown in the treadling sequence.

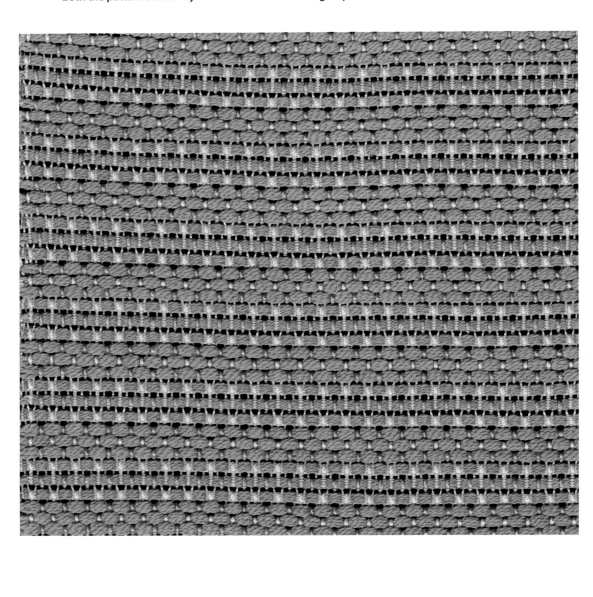

322-5

	1	2	3	4	5	6	a	b
	4	4			4			4
	3			3		3	3	
			2	2	2	2		2
		1	1		1	1	1	1

Weft

- ■ Pattern 1: 10/3 cotton delft blue
- □ Pattern 2: 10/3 cotton yellow
- ■ Tabby: 50/3 light olive drab

plain weave/tabby

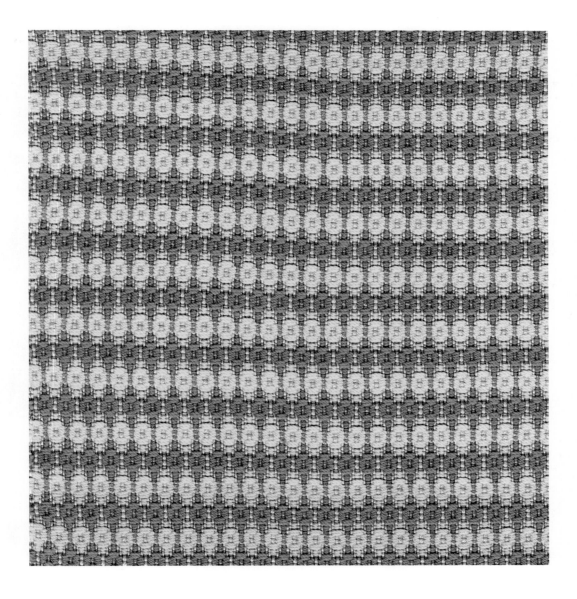

322-6

1	2	3	4	a	b
4	4				4
3			3	3	
		2	2		2
	1	1		1	

Weft

■ **Pattern: very dark green wool**
□ **Tabby: 50/3 light aqua**

□ plain
□ weave/tabby

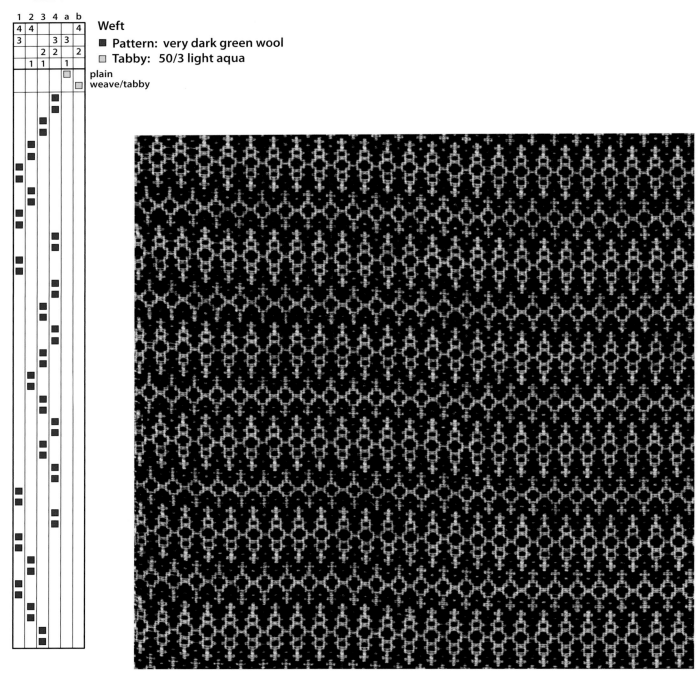

322-7

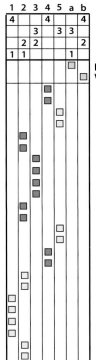

Weft

- ■ Pattern 1: 10/3 cotton medium green
- ☐ Pattern 2: 10/3 cotton cream
- ☐ Tabby: 50/3 gray beige

plain
weave/tabby

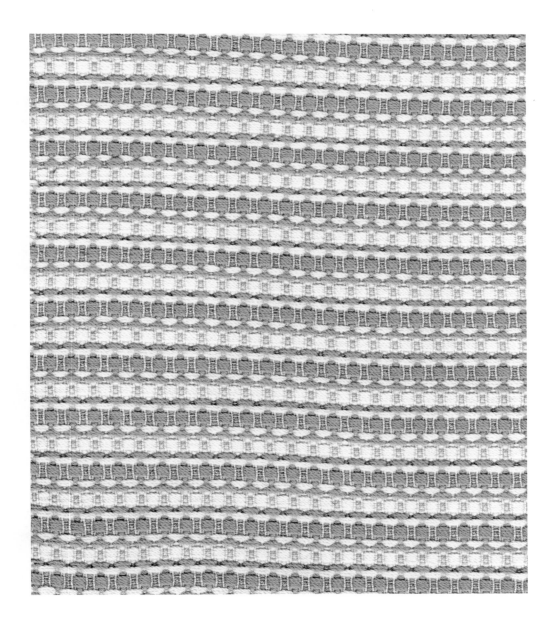

Warp 323A

Weave: Six-shaft Overshot

Sett: 30 epi

Warp: □ #30 crochet cotton beige

Threading repeat

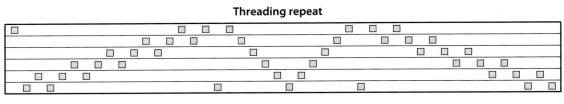

323A-3

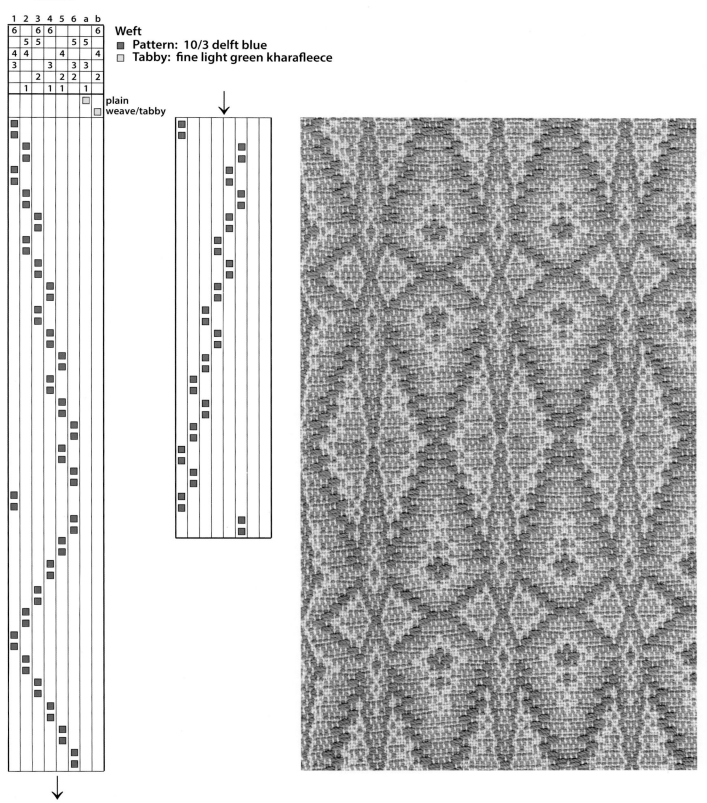

Weft
- ■ Pattern: 10/3 delft blue
- □ Tabby: fine light green kharafleece

plain weave/tabby

323A-4

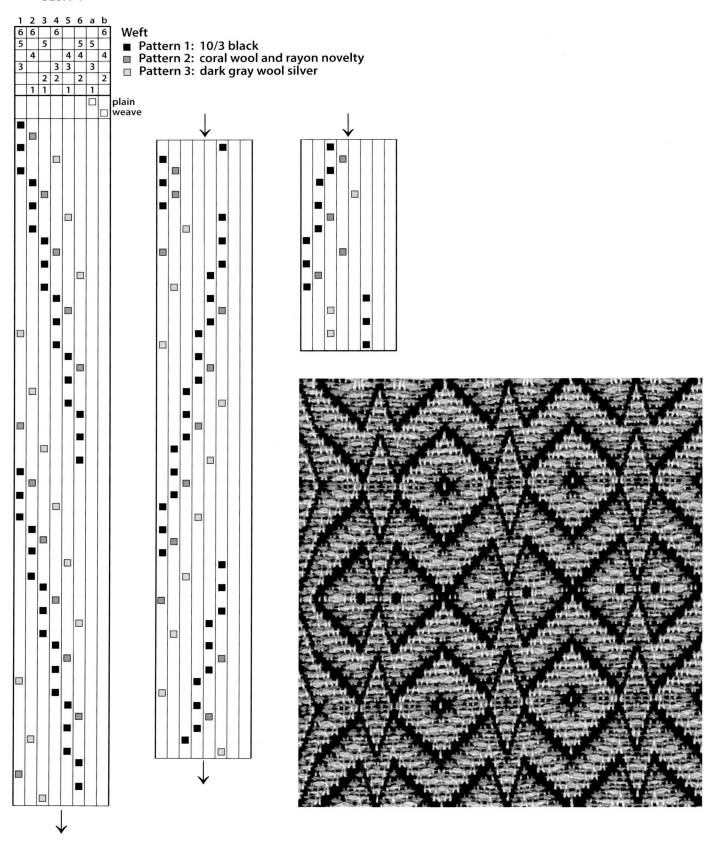

Weft

- ■ Pattern 1: 10/3 black
- ▨ Pattern 2: coral wool and rayon novelty
- ☐ Pattern 3: dark gray wool silver

☐ plain
☐ weave

323A-5

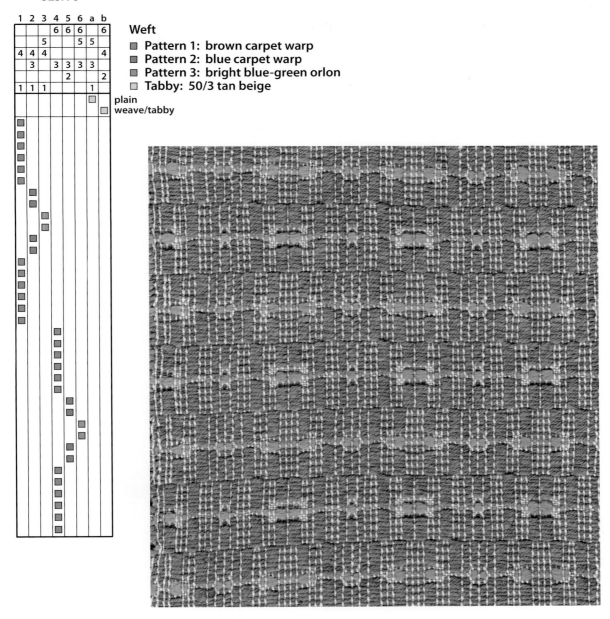

Weft

- ■ Pattern 1: brown carpet warp
- ■ Pattern 2: blue carpet warp
- ■ Pattern 3: bright blue-green orlon
- □ Tabby: 50/3 tan beige

323A-6

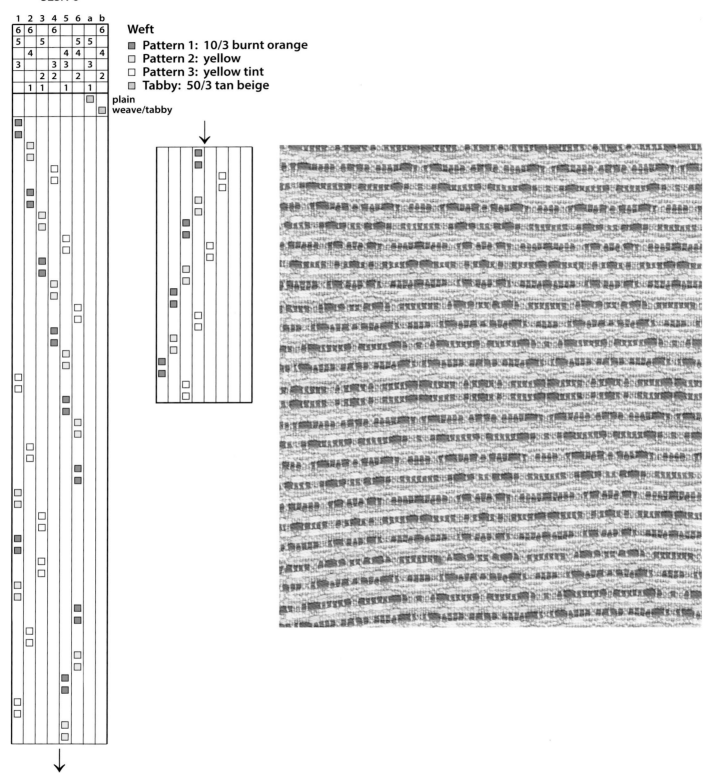

Weft

■ Pattern 1: 10/3 burnt orange
□ Pattern 2: yellow
□ Pattern 3: yellow tint
■ Tabby: 50/3 tan beige

plain
weave/tabby

Warp 362

Weave: Four-shaft Overshot
Sett: 37½ epi
Warp: ☐ 60/3 deep beige

Threading repeat

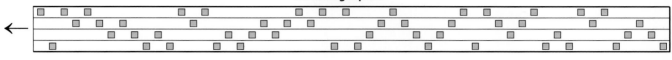

362-1

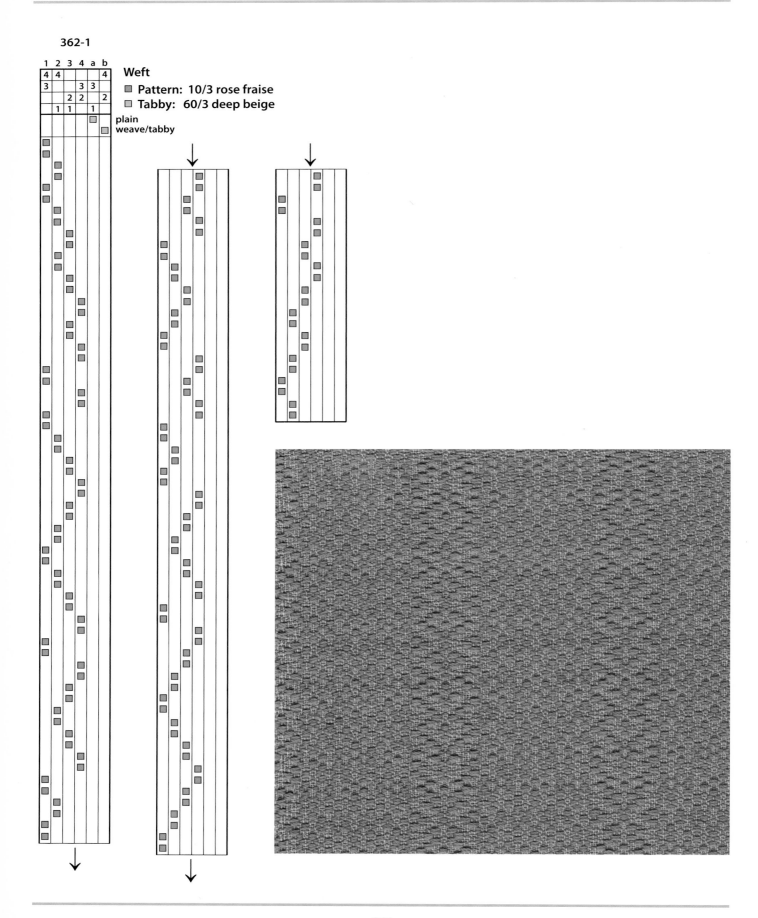

Weft

☐ Pattern: 10/3 rose fraise

☐ Tabby: 60/3 deep beige

362-2

1	2	3	4	a	b
4	4				4
3			3	3	
		2	2		2
	1	1		1	

plain
weave/tabby

Weft

■ Pattern: 10/3 brown

□ Tabby: 50/3 golden beige

362-6

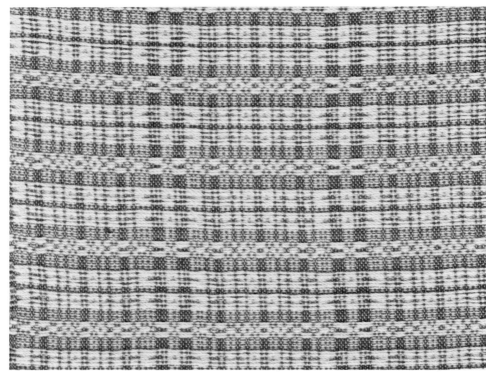

Weft

☐ **Pattern: 10/3 yellow**

■ **Tabby: 70/3 brown**

plain
weave/tabby

Warp 153

Weave: Four-shaft Swedish Lace
Sett: 22½ epi
Warp: ☐ 20/2 oyster linen

Threading repeat

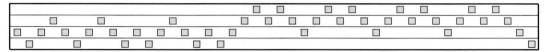

153-1

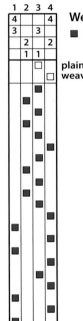

Weft
■ **Pattern: dark blue linen**

plain
weave

153-2

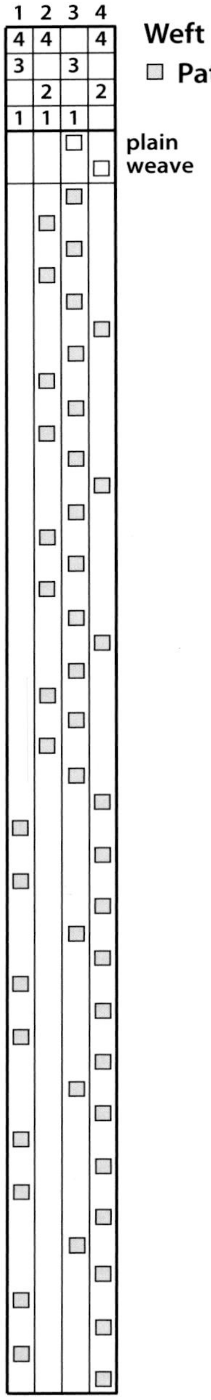

Weft

☐ Pattern: 20/2 oyster linen

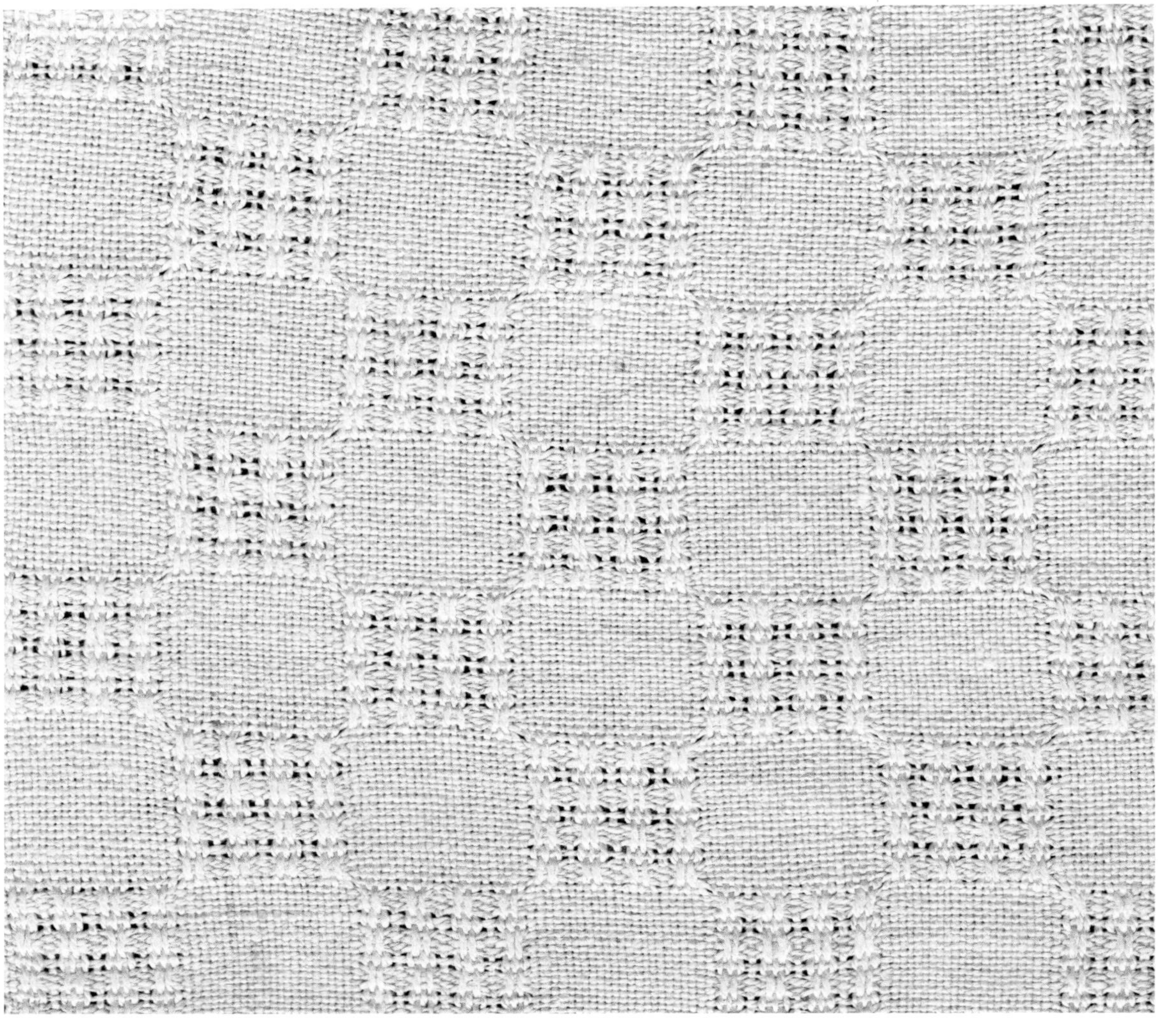

☐ plain weave

INDEX OF SAMPLES

ABOUT THE AUTHORS

 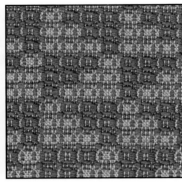 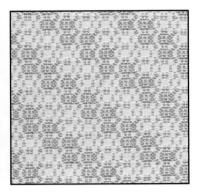

Robyn Spady, Nancy A. Tracy, and Marjorie Fiddler are hand weavers and members of the Seattle Weavers' Guild, one of the largest guilds in the US. Spady began weaving in 1969. She is a master weaver and travels extensively teaching a wide variety of programs and workshops. Tracy is active in several local guilds, as well as the international Complex Weavers organization. She has over 25 years of experience and her particular interest is in the structures of woven cloth and the looms that create them. She was fortunate to have been a friend of Virginia Harvey, who did the original work on publishing Dr. William Bateman's material. Fiddler is an award-winning weaver and dyer known for her striking use of color and exceptional craftsmanship.